A SKETCH OF CHURCH HISTORY

by

H. MORLEY RATTENBURY, M.A.

LONDON : THE EPWORTH PRESS

FIRST PUBLISHED IN 1962

© THE EPWORTH PRESS 1962

Book Steward
FRANK H. CUMBERS

SET IN MONOTYPE BASKERVILLE AND PRINTED IN
GREAT BRITAIN BY THE CAMELOT PRESS LTD
LONDON AND SOUTHAMPTON

A SKETCH OF CHURCH HISTORY

FOR

THE FAMILY

Contents

PREFACE 9

1 THE FIRST FIVE HUNDRED YEARS 11
The Growth of the Church. Persecution and
Triumph. Other Opposition. Disputes within the
Church. Tools for the Job.

2 THE DARK AGES, A.D. 500–950 . . 37
The Course of the Struggle. Byzantine Christianity.
Churches of the East. The Church of the West.

3 THE MIDDLE AGES, A.D. 950–1350 . 49
Advance. The Church in the West. Eastern
Churches.

4 THE TWILIGHT OF THE MIDDLE
AGES, A.D. 1350–1500 . . . 61
Christianity in the East. Christianity in the West.

5 THE MODERN CHURCH, A.D. 1500–1960 69
The Reformation and Its Consequences. The
Counter-Reformation and the Development of
Roman Catholicism. The Eastern Orthodox
Church. The Expansion of the Church. The
Ecumenical Movement.

POSTSCRIPT 103

BOOKS FOR FURTHER READING . 105

INDEX 107

Preface

THIS BOOK has grown from a short set of lectures given at the Institute of Education in the University of Leeds. Material used in other lectures and talks has been added. The appreciation shown by some listeners has suggested that a brief outline of Church History, such as is attempted here, may not be without use, especially for those who have never tried to see Church History as a whole.

One is tempted to say that there is little point in trying to tell the story of the Church in a matter of thirty thousand words, and, of course, the attempt to summarize the story briefly entails a quite ruthless selection of material. At the same time, there is some value in the effort, if only to present a broad idea of the main outline and proportion of the story.

This present attempt may perhaps be criticized as giving too much space to the first five hundred years. As Church History expands the importance of the early Church necessarily decreases in one sense. Yet, because the earliest years are so important in setting the pattern for the future and because, even in the modern world, younger churches may still have to share some of the experiences of the past, it has seemed right to give almost a third of the whole length to this period.

Reference to other books has been omitted from the text, partly in order to keep the book within the prescribed length. Consultation of too many books in the process of writing would only have reminded the writer of facts which had been conveniently forgotten, and the task of compression would have become impossible! The list of books given at the end, however, may prove helpful for further reading, and will indicate the indebtedness of the author to others.

CHAPTER ONE

The First Five Hundred Years

IN THE YEAR 410 Rome was sacked by the Goths. This was the first of the mortal blows which Germanic invaders continued to deliver against the Roman Empire for many years. The result was the break-up of the Empire so that only a shadow of its former glory remained at the end of the fifth century A.D. Yet throughout this period the missionary work of the Christian Church continued. Patrick, for instance, landed in Ireland as a missionary in the year 432. What, then, was the position of the Church about the year 500, when the Empire which had come to protect it had fallen?

THE GROWTH OF THE CHURCH

In the first five hundred years Christianity had spread throughout the Roman Empire. There were Christians in Spain, France, Britain and the other European countries south of the Rhine-Danube frontier, in Asia Minor, Syria, Palestine, Egypt and North Africa. Beyond the borders of the Empire missionary work had been carried on among the Germanic tribes themselves. Though this work had largely been undertaken by men judged unorthodox by the Church of the Empire, it softened the blow of the invaders, as Augustine pointed out in *The City of God*, and prepared the way for the acceptance of Christianity by the invaders when they settled within the Empire. In other countries, too—Persia, Armenia, Ethiopia, Ireland and Scotland—Christian communities had been established. And there is evidence of Christian groups in Arabia, India and Ceylon—partly, according to tradition, the result of the preaching of the apostle Thomas, partly perhaps the consequence of Christians seeking refuge from persecution in the countries of the Near East.

In only one place, namely around Carthage, had there been a setback to this extensive growth of the Church, but it was a decisive one. The church of Carthage had had a remarkable history. In time of persecution it had produced noble martyrs —Perpetua, for instance, the mother of an infant child, and Felicitas, the slave whose child was born in prison. It had produced outstanding leaders—Tertullian, Cyprian and Augustine of Hippo. But unfortunately it had fallen into party strife over matters of discipline and of the relationship between Church and State. Personal rivalries had added fuel to the flames, and there were the long-standing, almost nationalistic prejudices of local Africans against the central authority in Rome. The church parties, Catholics and Donatists, were thus involved in a very tangled situation. Matters became much worse when one of the rivals in the civil strife which broke out in Africa as the Roman Empire began to break up called in the Vandals to fight for him. From the Church's point of view this was disastrous, because the Vandals set out to destroy Christianity. Even now the Church has not reclaimed the ground then lost.

Apart from this very serious setback, however, the Church had achieved a great success. She survived the shambles of the Roman Empire in the fifth century, and more and more ordinary men and women came to look to her for protection when other protectors failed. This triumph of the Church had been secured against tremendous odds.

PERSECUTION AND TRIUMPH

In the early days Christians very soon proved the truth of their Lord's word that He had come to bring not peace but a sword. Every man's hand seemed to be against them. The Jews stirred up trouble wherever they could against people whom they thought to be blasphemers. Mobs in the cities turned against these dangerous innovators. Vested interests, like those of the silversmiths of Ephesus whose livelihood depended upon the worship at the temple of Diana, bitterly resented those who threatened to undermine their sources of income. In an increasing number of centres Christians were presenting a series of problems which threatened public order and, as an inevitable consequence, the State had to take cognisance of the situation.

While the Christians remained comparatively few in number, it was sufficient to deal with each incident as it arose. Local officials would take the usual measures adopted against disturbers of the peace, and the case of Paul must not be taken as typical. From the outset this case of the conversion of a prominent Jew to the new faith had all the makings of a *cause célèbre*, and everybody concerned—including Paul himself—made the most of it. How often, as in this case, the Christian problem came to the attention of the imperial courts in Rome is not known, but, when it did, the action of an emperor like Claudius (41-54) is probably more typical. During his reign there appear to have been disturbances between Jews and Christians in Rome itself. Claudius adopted the simple measure of expelling all 'Jews' from the city, as though this were simply an incident confined to the ancient problem of the relations of the Jews with the Empire—a measure which suggests that there was some confusion in the minds of the authorities and that they did not recognize the nature of the new problem. Similarly the actions of the emperors Nero (54-68) and Domitian (81-96), though brutal enough for those who had to suffer from them, do not indicate any settled policy on the part of the government towards the Christians. These rulers seem to have continued to rely on 'information received' and on sporadic police raids. The popular tradition that they were the worst persecutors of the Church can be explained by reference to early Christian writings as well as to modern novels and films, but it is hardly in accordance with the facts.

It is at the beginning of the second century that a new note can be detected in Roman official documents. By this time the Christian communities in a few areas had grown so large that it seemed as though they might soon form the majority of the local population. This was perhaps especially so in Asia Minor where the Christian mission to the Gentiles had had so amazing a success from the time of Paul onwards. It was from this quarter that Pliny the Younger, governor of Bithynia, wrote to the emperor for advice in the year 112. Like other governors he had been taking steps against the Christians, but the problem had now become so acute that he wanted to know whether the emperor approved what he was doing and whether the steps he was taking were thought to be adequate. The Christians were showing 'pertinacity and inflexible obstinacy' —contempt of court—and they seemed prey to 'nothing but a depraved and extravagant superstition'. He had made careful enquiries concerning the nature of the new religion— though it is clear from the details he gives that the whole business is still beyond the comprehension of a sober Roman official—and, in particular, he wanted to know whether he was right in meting out capital punishment. His policy so far had secured a better attendance at temples which had become almost deserted.

The emperor Trajan (98-117) approved of Pliny's policy. The only thing he set his face against was the employment of informers and anonymous pamphlets. But, if Christians were properly charged and brought to trial, the only thing that could save them was recantation and 'worshipping our gods'. He commended Pliny's careful examination of each case, 'for no hard and fast rule can be laid down, of universal application', and the correspondence on both sides is an excellent example of the high standards of Roman justice at its best. It is sometimes argued that Trajan's instructions inaugurated a more peaceful period for the Church, because they protected Christians from the 'slanderous informers' and 'clamorous demands and outcries' to which his successor Hadrian (117-38) referred when he, in his turn, came to issue similar instructions to one of his governors. But it is equally clear that, provided proper legal procedure was followed, both emperors were definitely of the opinion that the obstinate confession of Christianity was a capital crime (there was, after all, a hint of treason about it, since Christians would not worship the Roman Emperor), and no

Christian properly tried could hope to escape the full penalty of the law. The same policy seems to have continued in the reign of the next emperor, Antoninus Pius (138-61), who gained a reputation for mildness by restraining the over-zealousness of some of the attacks on Christians in Greece, but whose reign nevertheless saw the opposition to Christianity continue.

In this period the most famous of many martyrdoms were those of Ignatius of Antioch and Polycarp of Smyrna. Ignatius was permitted to make what amounted to a triumphal progress through Asia Minor to Rome, where he was thrown to the beasts in the arena. On his way he met or wrote to many Christians, infecting them with his own good courage. In particular he wrote to the Christians in Rome begging them not to make any attempt to use their influence on his behalf. 'I die willingly for God. . . . Suffer me to belong to the wild beasts, through whom I may attain to God. I am God's grain, and I am ground by the teeth of wild beasts, that I may be found pure bread.' Polycarp was an old man when he was taken to his trial, but to all the threats and persuasions that were used against him he replied: 'Eighty and six years have I served Him and He did me no wrong. How shall I blaspheme my King who has saved me?' Stories of men like these were passed round the churches and their influence can well be imagined.

But, if the story and example of the martyrs served to stiffen the resistance of the Church to persecution, the effect on some Romans was very different. To Marcus Aurelius the Stoic emperor (161-80) the attitude of men like Ignatius to martyr-dom was exhibitionist and contemptible. Death should be faced quietly and privately, not publicly and with glorification. Moreover the emperor was faced with the fact that the steps so far taken to deal with the Christians were proving inadequate. Their numbers were increasing and people were beginning to say that the troubles of the Empire—flood, fire, plague and war—were due to the anger of the gods against the increasing influence of the 'atheists'. In this reign, therefore, because

B

the emperor was a noble character seriously concerned about the Roman way of life, attacks on the Christians increased in severity. There is evidence of martyrdoms from all quarters of the Empire—Gaul, Rome, Asia Minor and Africa—and, in addition to the normal processes of law which continued, the emperor was prepared to countenance the use of public trial and torture. The classic example of this was in the year 177 when, in two towns in Gaul, Lyons and Vienne, some fifty Christians were submitted to prolonged and intense torture of all kinds before being finally put to death. The victims ranged from an aged bishop to a slave, Blandina, and her fifteen-year-old brother, who were the last two victims. Blandina had to watch her brother die and then, after lengthy torture, was herself gored to death by a bull. Incidentally, it is possible that refugees from this persecution in Gaul were among the first who brought Christianity to Britain. At any rate there were Christians in Britain before the end of the second century, long before the main conversion of the country in the sixth and seventh centuries, and before the later date the Christian community had already produced its first saint, Alban, and its first heretic, Pelagius!

Fortunately for the Christians the full fury of this kind of persecution was not maintained by all the emperors. Septimius Severus (193-211) tried another policy by forbidding both Jews and Christians to proselytize their faith. In other words, he sought to reduce the number of those adopting the new faith. But for one reason and another, chiefly preoccupation with other affairs of state, it was not until halfway through the third century that the government at last embarked on a comprehensive attempt to stamp out the Church.

By this time the Church had grown further both in numbers and in organization. The State was now being seriously challenged by an illegal society of considerable strength and decisive steps had to be taken. Two emperors, Decius (249-51) and Valerian (254-9), were responsible for the new policy which was to be applied officially, universally and systematically. Every local magistrate was involved and a definite date was fixed for the inauguration of the attack. Christians were to be arrested and those who refused to sacrifice on the imperial altar were to be imprisoned and tortured until they consented to sacrifice. The object of the attack was not to put Christians to death but to secure a wholesale return to Roman ways, nevertheless many of the victims died. A graduated code of punishment was drawn up for the various ranks of society, and special efforts were made to persuade the leaders of the Church, the bishops, to recant. It is obvious that, if the State could have secured a large number of recantations from the Christian leaders, great propaganda use could have been made of their apostasy. Once again, however, the government was faced, on the whole, by an unbreakable spirit of constancy and courage. During this period, for instance, five bishops of Rome were martyred, and the see was actually vacant at one period for sixteen months.

Whether this policy, if persisted in, would have resulted in the almost wholesale destruction of the Church was never proved. A series of troubles, internal and external, struck the Empire, and it was not until Diocletian and his co-regents had achieved a thorough reorganization of the Empire (284-313) that the government could give attention once more to the religious problem. In the interval the missionary work of the Church had been going steadily on. The ground lost in the earlier attack had been more than recovered. The Church had by this time acquired property—the most remarkable building in Diocletian's capital, Nicomedia, was a Christian church—and the emperor's wife and daughter, as well as some of his advisers, were adherents, if not members, of the faith.

It seems possible that Diocletian himself did not want to press a new attack upon the Church, but he was eventually over-persuaded by others, and, although he set his face against imposing a death penalty, in 303 there began a persecution of Christians which was to prove the most thorough and severe ever. A series of edicts ordered the destruction of churches and Christian writings, decreed loss of rank and enslavement for various classes of Roman citizens, and insisted on the arrest of all clergy. This policy, universally applied, soon resulted in prisons being filled to overflowing. Torture followed, and finally Christians were offered the alternative of sacrificing or accepting death with the confiscation of property.

Once again what would have been the results of this policy if it had been long maintained will never be known. The rulers in the eastern half of the Empire persisted with the persecution for some time, but the Church was saved by the rise to power of Constantine in the west. There has been a great deal of argument about the motives which dictated the newcomer's policy. Some have argued that the favour he showed Christians was a political move only, that he wanted the support of Christians in his bid for power. But this view perhaps exaggerates the influence of Christians at this date, ignores the Christian influences that may already have been brought to bear upon him in the circles in Britain in which he had been brought up, and hardly gives due weight to the interest he took in Church affairs throughout his reign. His policy, which had to be carefully conducted because of the large number of pagans still in the Empire, was certainly favourable towards the Christians, and he himself was baptized at the last on his death bed.

Whatever the motives of Constantine (313-37), the position of the Church was completely changed under him and his son Constantius (337-61). The Edict of Milan in 313 granted the same freedom of worship to Christians as to the followers of other religions, and restored to the Church property which had been confiscated during the persecution. Under imperial protection the Church was tremendously strengthened, and the attempt of Julian (361-3) to restore paganism only served to show how strong Christianity now was and how impossible it was to put the clock back. The reign of Theodosius (379-95) saw the virtual end of paganism as the official religion of the Empire, and the career of a bishop like Ambrose of Milan (340-97) is a good illustration of the new stature now attained by churchmen. Here was a leading Christian who had sufficient authority to withstand evil policies in imperial circles, to advise and even to reprove the emperor himself; and ordinary people looked more and more to men of this calibre to protect them against injustice and bad government.

Yet the triumph of Christianity was not without its new problems. Though the tendency should not be exaggerated, it is undoubtedly true that the protected Church offered new avenues of advancement to those who were concerned only with securing imperial favour. A most unpleasant atmosphere of intrigue and backstairs diplomacy enters into Church affairs at some levels. The whole question of the new relationship between Church and State had to be worked out afresh. To some, like the Donatists in Africa, it appeared that the emperor was interfering in matters that were none of his business. But other Christians deliberately sought the protection of the State and thought that it was part of the business of a Christian emperor at least to advise in Church affairs. The difficulty of the new situation is illustrated by the shock of horror that went through the Church when, in the year 384, a Christian, Priscillian, was executed for heresy. The events which led to this execution are involved and tangled by intrigue, but this first use of the death penalty in Church affairs was, at least, an ominous foretaste of things to come.

Yet when all has been said that can be said of the difficulties and dangers that came to the Church when it was recognized by the State, this fact remains: all the might of Rome had proved insufficient to stamp out the new religion. Against all the odds, as Julian said, the Galilean had conquered.

OTHER OPPOSITION

The opposition of the government was not the only obstacle which the Church had to overcome. Christianity represented a challenge to a very great deal in the whole life of Roman society and religion, and the dangers which Christians faced were by no means confined to the public courts, the prisons and the arenas. As on the mission field today, so in the Roman Empire, a man who became a Christian was liable to find himself cut off immediately from home and friends. It was impossible for one who was a Christian to take part in many of the activities of pagan society, and so he found himself an outcast, relying for support only on the handful of others in similar circumstances. 'A man's foes shall be they of his own household.' And this is why Paul and other early Christian writers are so often concerned with collections for the poor and with the Christian duty of hospitality. If Christians did not support one another no one else would care for them. To the rest of the world they were as good as dead.

It was this separation of the Christians from the rest of society which accounted for many of the accusations levelled against the new faith. To the pagan world it was a horrible and dangerous novelty. The Christians were atheists because they refused to worship the gods whom others worshipped. They were traitors because they refused to worship at the imperial shrines. They were thought to be guilty of all sorts of immoral practices at their secret meetings. They were unpatriotic, following apparently some other king than Caesar, and their views threatened the whole structure of society. Freemen and slaves, men and women, people of all races, were brought together in a society which was beyond the understanding of the typical Roman citizen. They had unbelievable, strange superstitions. All this brought the anger of the gods upon the Empire, and every calamity was laid at their door. As Tertullian wrote: 'If Tiber rises to the walls, if Nile does not rise to the fields, if the sky stands still, if the earth moves, if there is famine, if there is plague . . . the cry is: The Christians to the lions!'

All this sort of criticism of Christianity was summed up in the work of a man called Celsus, who had made some study of both Judaism and Christianity and whose attack on the Christians was, therefore, better informed than some. He questioned the teaching of the Church. If its message was true, why did God leave it so late to come to the rescue of the world? God could not do anything that was not perfect, was it not, then, blasphemy to suggest that God's creation needed saving? If God were to send a saviour, was it credible that he would send him to such an obscure part of the Empire as Judaea and to such a despised people as the Jews? What about the contradictions in the sacred writings of the Christians? And so on. And above all, Celsus appealed to the patriotism of the Christians. Could they not see that their views were threatening to split the Empire, that they were already bringing down the wrath of the gods upon the people? Let them worship in their own way, if they chose, but let them compromise as others did and not keep themselves to themselves.

It was through suffering this sort of opposition that Christians learnt that they had to undertake the enormous task of explaining their faith to the world in which they lived, and so there came into being the work of Christian apologists. Men like Justin Martyr, Tertullian and Origen set out to give the Christian answer to criticism. They did it in public as well as in private, and the success that attended their work is confirmed by the extraordinary number of people who seem to have undergone an intellectual conversion. The Church was learning that it had to satisfy the heads as well as the hearts of men.

This can be further seen in the successful answer which the Church gave to the other religions and philosophies of the day. The Roman Empire was a melting-pot of ideas. Out of the bringing together of many peoples from east and west there came a groping after the worship of one god, and various religions such as those of Serapis and Isis from Egypt and of Mithras—a kind of sun-worship—were being advanced as a compendium of all religion. The mystery religions were seeking to satisfy man's desire for cleansing and for some assurance of immortality. Manicheism was an attempt to explain the problem of evil and the way of salvation from it. Philosophers were in great vogue and some of them acted rather like private chaplains in great houses, while others wandered from place to place offering the consolation of their teaching in the market-place and at street corners. The noblest philosophies like Neo-Platonism and Stoicism set before men a high conception of eternal realities beyond this life or a high standard of duty for this life. But the Gnostics only offered a weird amalgam of eastern, Jewish and Christian teaching together with strange explanations of creation and the nature of evil. To be saved one required to find a special key to knowledge, and it was obvious that this was not to be revealed to everybody. There was little hope in this sort of teaching for the world at large.

Religions and philosophies like these could come in all sorts of shapes and sizes, and the melting-pot produced all manner of modifications of the original models. For many ordinary people of the day, religion would, no doubt, consist largely of what came nearest to hand: the local temple or shrine, whatever that happened to be, some traditional family practices, and perhaps a little emperor worship thrown in on State occasions. But never before had there been the possibility of such traffic in ideas as the Roman Empire, by bringing so many races so closely together, had provided.

The temptation for the Church was to join in the game, to borrow and exchange ideas, to compromise, and in the great debate there were ideas discovered in other religions and philosophies which could be put to Christian use. But on the main question there could be no compromise. However illiberal it might seem to others, the Church had to insist that only the truth could set men free. The truth that had been revealed to Christians was the truth that came by Jesus Christ. It was on this historic basis that Christian theologians took their stand, and, whether they claimed, as they sometimes did, that all that was good in other ways of thought belonged to them or whether they stated, as they did at other times, that Christians had no need of philosophy, they were clear at all times that the word of Christ was the final word of God.

So men like Justin Martyr in Rome, Tertullian in Carthage, Clement and Origen in Alexandria, Augustine in Hippo, set out to show the world that the Christian faith was intellectually respectable and, indeed, superior to the alternatives. The proclamation of the truth might be an offence to many, but in the end it was Christ and all that flowed from Him that alone satisfied what men had been groping for in other religions and philosophies. Some of these men only came to the acceptance of Christian truth after a long intellectual and spiritual pilgrimage—Justin and Augustine in particular have left accounts of this—but, in the end, they knew this was the only answer. In the clash of debate which ensued it was the old ways of thought that faded away, not the 'dangerous novelty'.

DISPUTES WITHIN THE CHURCH

At the same time that the dispute with the world outside was going on, there was a parallel and even prior discussion taking place within the Church itself. Already in very early days, as the New Testament makes clear, it was possible for there to be different apprehensions of Christian truth, and by the beginning of the second century, especially under the influence of Gnostic opinions, there seemed a danger that quite dissimilar interpretations of Christianity might arise. The Church began, therefore, to look for a *regula fidei*—a rule of faith—which, without being an absolutely rigid codification of truth, was yet a generally received summary of history and scripture, confirmed by tradition and reason, handed down from generation to generation and expressing the common experience of the majority of Christians. In the early days this did not involve the Church in anything like a prolonged heresy hunt, but, as argument mounted, it became clear that some sort of formulation of the faith was necessary in order to make clear the limits within which the thought of Christians might move without fear of compromise with the truth. One of the first to give the Church something to think about was Marcion, son of the bishop of Sinope, a port on the Black Sea. He arrived in Rome in 140, and was at first well received because of his generous gifts to the church there. But he was soon startling his fellow Christians with his strange views, his gifts were returned to him, and he was being called 'the first-born of Satan'. The trouble was that he appears to have been so convinced of the absolute uniqueness of Christianity that he tried to sever it completely from its roots in Judaism. The God of the Old Testament, he maintained, was quite a different Being from the God and Father of our Lord Jesus Christ; the One was a God of justice, the Other of mercy, and there could be no reconciliation between the two ideas. He proposed, therefore, that Christians should abandon the use of the Jewish scriptures, and that, of the new Christian writings which were being circulated, the Church should only accept a truncated version of St Luke's Gospel and the Pauline epistles —all references to the Old Testament were to be deleted. We shall see that this 'criticizing with a pen-knife', as it was called, was to have some effect upon the growth of the New Testament. Meanwhile it is sufficient to note that the Church rejected these views which cut so drastically at the belief that Christ lived and suffered 'according to the scriptures'. The Church's roots, it was claimed, were firmly fixed in the past, and the God who offered salvation through Jesus Christ was the same God who had been Redeemer for all ages.

Another innovator was Montanus, who also flourished in the second century. His teaching was that a new age of the Holy Spirit had begun. The Paraclete spoke through him and his attendant prophets and prophetesses, and the New Jerusalem was about to descend on a village in Phrygia called Pepuza. The expected event did not take place, but Montanus and his followers continued to propagate their views, and in their exaggerated way they were, of course, bearing witness to Christian belief in the work of the Holy Spirit. But the Church could not welcome a movement which challenged the properly constituted authorities of the Christian body and relied solely upon ecstatic utterances and meaningless 'speaking with tongues'. Nor could it accept that the new revelation supplanted the historic revelation in Jesus Christ. The Christian Faith must be grounded in history. So long as the Montanists remained a 'ginger group' within the Church— as they did in Africa—reminding Christians of the need to 'watch and pray', there was perhaps a place for them, but, when they permitted themselves to indulge in silly pentecostalism, their views had to be rejected.

A third group of views which arose in the second and third centuries brought into question the trinitarian language that was being used in the Church. To many it seemed that to worship in the name of Christ or the Holy Spirit detracted from the Oneness of God, and some accused the Christians of worshipping three gods. The Monarchians, therefore, insisted that God is One and that the only proper way to think of Jesus was either as a man so good that he was eventually adopted into the Godhead, or as merely a temporary appearance of God—a part that He played for the time being for the purpose of saving the world. The trouble with these views was that neither of them gave a picture of Jesus Christ 'the same yesterday, today and for ever'. A mere man, however good, is unable to save mankind, and a God who merely acted the part of a man could not be said really to have suffered for us men and for our salvation. Moreover, some of the advocates of these views did not commend them by their lives. For instance, Paul of Samosata, bishop of Antioch, was known to be over fond of feminine flattery, and was not above feeling pleasure at applause for his sermons in church. Sabellius also, one of the other leaders of the Monarchians, was so unpopular for his views that later theologians were anxious at all costs to avoid the accusation of being called 'Sabellians'.

But the disputes of the first three centuries paled into insignificance beside the far more bitter disputes of the next two centuries. Unhappily it appeared that, once the opposition of the State was removed, Christians turned instead against each other. Rivalries between various sees and schools of thought came to the surface, and there were even cases of bribery and corruption being employed in order to secure support for rival church parties. At the same time, however, principles of fundamental importance were involved. Now that Christianity was a recognized religion, it was important that its teaching should be exactly defined so that false prophets should not arise to claim the protection now offered to the Christians. Moreover, the earlier disputes had shown that there was a real need to state the implications of belief in Christ, and to have a clear statement concerning His person.

In these circumstances the views of Arius, a presbyter of Alexandria, caused an explosion. Against the advice of his bishop, he started publicizing his view that, though it might be right to use certain New Testament phrases which seemed to suggest that Jesus was divine, his divinity was, in fact, only second class. God and God only is truly divine. His Son must be subordinate to Him and created by Him. Of Jesus one could say, therefore, that there was a time when he was not. In other words he was not eternal. If he was not eternal, he was not really God. It may have been that, like the Monarchians, Arius was concerned to safeguard the unity of God, but Athanasius, another presbyter in Alexandria, took the view that Arius' explanation was not the only one possible. He argued that the Word of God must have been with God from the beginning. Only the eternal Word of God was capable of saving mankind, and it was by the incarnation of His eternal Word that God had, in fact, reconciled the world to Himself. On this view Jesus could be thought of as eternally divine. So the battle was joined.

The dispute became so heated that, at length, the Emperor had to intervene for the sake of peace and order. In 325 he summoned what was to prove to be the first of a series of Councils of the Church, at Nicea, and he personally encouraged the theologians to settle their dispute. Briefly, the outcome of the Council was that the views of Athanasius were vindicated and that Arius and a few of his supporters were exiled. The Council produced a Creed, the first statement of its kind which could be held to be binding on all Christians, and it included the phrase that Christ was of one substance with the Father. This phrase involved the use of a doubtful, non-scriptural word, and many of the bishops at Nicea would have liked to avoid it if it had been at all possible. But it was argued that this phrase alone would protect the teaching of the

Church from the perversions of Arius, and so, in the end, the Council agreed to the formula.

This was, however, by no means the end of the affair. Once the Creed of Nicea had been published, second thoughts were possible, and many of the bishops of the time were reluctant to admit that the new creed was any better than the formulas which they had been using in their various churches previously. This left plenty of room for manoeuvre of which the Arians were quick to take advantage, and there followed thirty-five years of dispute, argument and intrigue in an attempt to find a formula satisfactory to all. The desire for uniformity is, perhaps, the key to the situation, for Constantius followed his father Constantine in wanting the Church to come to a definite decision in this matter, and so was willing to listen to any party which could represent its views as the views of the majority. Moreover, for a long time many of the eastern bishops looked with disfavour on the views of Athanasius. His motives were questioned, he was frequently attacked and slandered, and he was on several occasions himself sent into exile. The Emperor, with his capital now in Constantinople, was particularly susceptible to the views of the eastern bishops. But, on the whole, Athanasius enjoyed the support of the West, and in the end the new generation of eastern bishops came to see that his views had, in fact, been correct and were the only safeguard against Arianism. So, after innumerable minor councils, another General Council was called at Constantinople in 361, and a revised and even more precise version of the Creed of Nicea was accepted, the creed which is now known as the Nicene Creed. A few years before, Athanasius himself had died, but the view that he had held against the world, so it seemed at one time, was ratified.

After Constantinople theological dispute shifted to slightly new ground. If Jesus was divine, the question arose as to how full divinity and full humanity could be combined in one person. The next series of councils, therefore, was mainly concerned with this matter and with the views of men like Apollinarius, Nestorius, and Eutyches, who proposed various answers to the problem. All their solutions were in the end rejected because in one way or another they detracted either from the full divinity or from the full humanity of Christ. The Church insisted that the Saviour must be fully divine in order to bring God to man, and fully human in order to bring man to God. No person who was less than both divine and human could be the Mediator and Redeemer. The Council of Chalcedon in 451 finally accepted a formula which asserted that Christ is both God and man, and so at last the faith of the Church was firmly grounded on the foundation of a Christ who is two natures in one person, One who is able to save to the uttermost.

Meanwhile, in contrast with these disputes, which were debated mainly in the east, another great controversy had arisen in the west. This was the controversy in which the main protagonists were Augustine and Pelagius, and it revolved round the questions of the nature of man and of his salvation. Augustine took the view that sin had so destroyed man that he is incapable of lifting a finger towards his own salvation. He introduced into Christian theology the first full statement of the doctrine of original sin, and taught, as a consequence, that salvation is offered only to those whom God, in His mercy, chooses, and for the rest there is no hope. Pelagius, on the other hand, took the view more commonly held hitherto that sin had not destroyed man, but only weakened him. With the advantage of the help of God, man remained, therefore, responsible for making some effort of his own towards salvation, and Pelagius urged Christians not to relax, but to work out their own salvation.

The controversy became increasingly bitter, though it never brought about as much intrigue as did the Arian question, and in the end the Pelagian party was defeated. The Church has always asserted that salvation is of God and that man cannot save himself. And though not all the most extreme statements that Augustinians have made have been generally accepted, the Church as a whole has always been in debt to Augustine for his clear statement of the fact that man owes everything to the grace of God.

One other controversy in which Augustine was involved also ought to be noticed, namely, his dispute with the Donatists. It has already been seen that this African sect was opposed to those who seemed to them to be falling too much under the influence of the State. Both persuasion and force were used in the attempt to bring these rigorists into communion with the rest of the Church, but they refused any kind of compromise, and the question at issue became more and more an argument concerning the nature of the Church itself. Augustine, developing arguments outlined by his great African predecessor, Cyprian, made it quite clear that he believed that the Church depended on her unity and upon the episcopal succession. Outside the Church there was no salvation. It was through the sacraments of the true Church alone that men were kept in the way of salvation. So this dispute between Christians led to a sharpening of the definition of the Church and, in particular, to doctrines which were further hardened in the Catholic Church of the Middle Ages.

TOOLS FOR THE JOB

From what has already been said, it is clear that through opposition and dispute the shape of the Church was clearly emerging in this period. But side by side with the great debates the normal inner life of the Church was also developing, and the missionary and pastoral work undertaken by Christians was as formative as any of the other matters so far considered. It was the whole process of witness, life and worship which made the Church what she became, and the importance of the first five hundred years is that in all aspects of her life an instrument was being forged for the purposes of God in the world. Christians were discovering the tools for the job. Quite apart from the disputes in which she was involved, the preaching and worship of the Church, the teaching of those who sought membership within the new community, and the service which Christians felt called to offer to society, all helped to bring the Church into being, and it is necessary now to note some of the processes by which this was achieved.

We have already noticed, for instance, how theological controversy emphasized the need for a statement of the Faith which could be used as a basis for distinguishing between those who held the Catholic, universal, beliefs of the Church and those who proposed some modification or other of the saving truth. But long before that historical necessity arose many churches were already using baptismal formulas in the training of new members of the Church. Men and women who wanted to become Christians had to be taught what Christian belief was, and the Creeds which eventually emerged from the great councils were based on these formulas of the Faith which arose from the sheer necessities of Christian preaching and instruction. The change which took place in the fourth and fifth centuries was that a universally accepted Creed of the Church was added to the formulas which previously had been designed merely for the needs of local churches. A great process of systematization took place in a region of the Church's life where previously there had been a good deal of freedom and speculation. This does not mean that there had been a great diversity earlier on. All formulas of belief had been based on the same tradition and Scriptures, as well as upon reason and a kind of enlightened common sense. But it is important to recognize that the teaching and pastoral work of the Church tended in the same direction as the requirements of theological argument, and that the Creed eventually produced was the result of a combination of needs.

The same is true of the production of the New Testament. In the process of the regular preaching and teaching of the Church certain writings gradually emerged as being of particular inspiration and authority. They came to be recognized as giving the clearest expression of the faith by which Christians lived, and this process of both divine and natural selection went on concurrently with the suggestion of a man like Marcion that a very narrow selection of Christian writings should be adopted. In answering Marcion, the Church fell back on writings already tested and proved, and so, once again, controversy and the normal life of the Church tended to the same end—in this case the production of the New Testament. This was to become the word of God for the infant Church, and the importance of this tool for the Church's work is underlined by the work undertaken by men like Origen of Alexandria and Jerome. The Vulgate edition of the Bible produced by Jerome in the fifth century, and still regarded as authoritative by the Roman Church, is witness of the care which was given to arriving at the most accurate text possible at the time and of the Church's concern that her message should be based on the given word of God and not upon writings and speculations of men.

At the same time, too, the Church was being given shape through her worship. In early days this would take place in the homes of Christians or in secret places where the Christians in a town could conveniently come together. By the third century, Christians were, in some places, setting aside special buildings for the purpose of worship, though it was not until after the recognition of Christianity by Constantine that the Church was really secure in her hold upon property. There was probably a certain amount of variety in worship at first, and it cannot be assumed that the evidence of one church is necessarily evidence of what went on throughout the Church as a whole. But the common background of Judaism and increasing intercommunication between the churches were influences which led to increasing uniformity, and it is clear that in any case Christian worship always centred around the reading of scriptures, preaching, and the two sacraments of Baptism and Eucharist. It did not take long, therefore, for the main outline of Christian worship to be established, and this process, as well as the mere preaching of the gospel as opportunity offered in public places, would have its effect upon the creed of the Church and her canon of scripture. It is clear from various pieces of evidence that the worship of the Church was not always established in all its purity—superstitious practices persisted in many places. But the Christian community was always a worshipping community, and it was part of the Church's missionary task to strive for a pattern of

C

worship which would worthily express its belief in God through Jesus Christ.

The growing life of the Church necessitated increasingly complex organization. Authority and control were needed, not only to resist attacks from outside and to safeguard the essential truths for which the Church stood, but also to give visible expression to the spiritual unity which bound the new international body into one. No clear system of church organization is outlined in the New Testament, and it is possible that there was some variety of development in the early days of the Church. But it is clear that by the second century the Church had discovered that an episcopal system best answered her immediate needs and that the members of the Church felt that this system was divinely inspired. Already, at the beginning of the century, Ignatius, bishop of Antioch—one of the more fully organized churches at this date—wrote: 'All of you follow the bishop as Jesus Christ followed the Father, and follow the presbytery as the Apostles; and respect the deacons as the commandment of God. Let no man perform anything pertaining to the church without the bishop.' And, although in other Christian communities 'prophets' seem to have been of higher authority than even the bishops, whom the people were bidden to choose for themselves, the episcopal system and the three-fold ministry increasingly proved its worth, and before the end of the century another writer, Hegesippus, is using the word 'succession' in connection with it. In those troubled times the bishop stood as the rallying point of Christian defence, as the guarantee of the traditions of the Church's teaching, and as the expression of the unity of Christians through their common Lord. In the centuries which followed, the life and organization of the Church developed in many ways. There were many differing ministries to be performed. But all the time the episcopal system and the three-fold ministry remained the core of whatever growth took place, and proved itself adaptable to many differing times and circumstances.

Linked with the growth of organization was the need of

maintaining discipline within the Church. This was occasioned first by the incidence of persecution, and later by the development of heresies, but all the time there was also, of course, the need to maintain the high standards of Christian character and conduct. Obviously those who had betrayed the cause in any way could not be allowed to make their own terms if they sought readmission to the Christian community, and from very early days three sins (apostasy, murder, and sexual immorality) were thought to be unforgivable. In other cases excommunication and penance—sometimes lifelong— were imposed as penalties. But this was a problem with which the Church was constantly struggling, and, as the pastoral concern of the Church grew, there was a tendency on the part of some at least to admit extenuating circumstances. Those who had lapsed during persecution began to be welcomed back into some churches if the bishop was satisfied that repentance was genuine, and, in general, there was a relaxation of some of the sterner penalties even in the grosser cases. The cause of this relaxation was, no doubt, a desire to win back the sinner rather than to condemn him for ever. But the growth of this 'Catholic' concern for the reclamation of those who had fallen brought about great disputes within the Church, since various rigorist parties felt that the standards of the Church were being betrayed. The rigorist protest was a proper reminder of the high standards required of Christians, but in general the Catholic view triumphed, and, under proper safeguards, repentant sinners were restored to Christian fellowship.

One of the centres agitated by this question of discipline was Rome, and the decisions of the Church there and the advice given to other churches were some of the means by which Rome came to have pre-eminence, especially in the West. But there were other reasons also. To be a Christian in Rome before the time of Constantine was always to live dangerously at the very heart of enemy country, and the survival of the church in Rome through the courage and faithfulness of all its members in all times of persecution was a symbol of the triumph which the whole Church was to win throughout the Empire. It was not long before Rome became naturally, along with Antioch, Alexandria, Carthage and, later, Constantinople, a centre of administration and missionary enterprise, and, especially in the West in the fourth and fifth centuries, she had no real rival. She was not so involved as the eastern centres were in the theological controversies which convulsed the Church in the East, and gained tremendous advantage from the attempts which were made by all parties to secure her support. This early period sees the emergence of the claim of the bishop of Rome to speak with the voice of St Peter, and this claim was sharpened by the rivalry which arose very early between Rome and Constantine's new capital. Constantinople claimed, as the new Rome, to have an authority equal to that of the ancient city, but this was a claim which Rome itself never allowed, and so the later split between East and West was already foreshadowed. In general the position seems to have been that other churches, although they gladly accorded to Rome a certain pre-eminence of honour, and were grateful for her support and for the inherited wisdom which she brought to the practical administration of affairs, were yet never prepared to acknowledge the absolute authority which she was beginning to claim. There are a number of cases in which the decision and advice of Rome were not accepted by churches in Africa, Asia Minor, Constantinople, and Alexandria. Even so, Leo I, bishop of Rome from 440 to 461, has been called 'the Father of the Papacy', and the foundations of later church history were already being laid.

One other important development of the first five centuries remains to be referred to, namely, the rise of monasticism. This is largely associated at first with the name of an Egyptian saint, Anthony, who inspired by the words, 'Go, sell that thou hast', committed himself to a life of asceticism and solitariness. The monk may be thought of as the Christian equivalent of the holy man of the East, and it is interesting that this new development in the life of the Church came at a time when the Church was becoming increasingly involved in politics and in the life of the world. The monk abandoned everything for a life of prayer and contemplation, not simply for his own salvation, but so that he might become a soldier of Christ, fighting the hosts of wickedness with spiritual weapons. At first the monks lived as hermits alone and apart from the world, but gradually groups of these hermits gathered round outstanding men like Anthony, and it was not long before community arrangements began to be made both for worship and for the common necessities of life. Much of the life was still, however, devoted to private spiritual exercises, and some of the monks were led into a rather unhealthy rivalry, seeking to establish, as it were, records in asceticism. From this and from the deserts where the first communities were established, monasticism was brought more fully into the life of the Church by the advice of men like Basil of Caesarea in Cappadocia. He persuaded monks to add social service to their other activities, and the hospital for the aged, poor and needy in the 'New City' outside the walls of Caesarea, and the two houses, one for men and one for women, which Jerome established at Bethlehem very largely to help him with his enormous literary output, were examples of the sort of service which the monastic orders were increasingly to render as time went on. In some centres, as in Ireland, the communities were also to become the spearhead of evangelism, though remaining essentially a movement for laymen.

The outline of the first five hundred years must end here. But enough has been said to show how tremendously important these years were. Not only were they sufficient to prove that the dangerous novelty was going to survive, but they also proved that the new faith was able to conquer. In conquering, the Church had begun to develop as an institution and to equip itself with the tools for its job. Christians were ready for the further shocks to come. When the Roman Empire went down in ruin in the fifth century, the Church was the only institution of that empire which survived, and it was the Church which preserved for the future the best of what Rome stood for. On Christmas Day, 496, Clovis, King of the

Franks, was baptized. This was the beginning of a new age which led to the establishment of Christendom, as it was known in the Middle Ages, the building up of the Roman Catholic Church, and the foundation of the Holy Roman Empire. And the triumphs of the Church were built, not only upon the achievements of its outstanding leaders, but also upon the work of countless ordinary men and women who have left no memorial but who kept the faith.

CHAPTER TWO

The Dark Ages, A.D. 500-950

THE CHURCH survived the fall of the Roman Empire, but it was touch and go, and the four and a half centuries which now concern us were a period of swaying fortunes and, indeed, of some loss of ground. Two attacks had to be faced, one from the north and north-east, the other from the south-east. The northern attack was that of the barbarian invasions, and it was not long before Visigoths were established in Spain, Ostrogoths in Italy, Burgundians in Southern Gaul, Vandals in North Africa, Anglo-Saxons in Britain, and Franks in Northern Gaul. Some of these tribes had already, as we have seen, had contact with Christianity, especially with what had been regarded as its heretical forms, and on the whole the Church was to prove successful in conquering the conquerors and bringing them into the true Faith. But in the south from the seventh century onwards, half of the Roman Empire passed into the control of the Arab conquerors and this loss involved the loss of much Christian territory to Islam. This loss was, therefore, the more serious, including as it did many of the old strongholds of Christianity, and it has never yet been made good.

THE COURSE OF THE STRUGGLE

When Rome itself fell, such remnants of Roman authority as survived tended to gather round the new Rome, Constantinople, which had been for some years the real centre of the government of the Empire. The rulers of Constantinople tried desperately to save what they could from the wreckage, and their efforts came to a peak in the reign of Justinian in the sixth century. Under this able leader imperial authority was restored in much of the East and in North Africa, and during this period also the Church made some attempt to make up for lost ground. Missionaries penetrated up the Nile into Sudan, and began a movement eastward which was to carry them in the following century as far as China. It was now, too, that the real conversion of Britain began with a twofold advance, first from Ireland and then from Rome. It is a great tribute to the missionary fervour of the Church that, so soon after the shocks of the barbarian invasions, she should be looking for new conquests, and Pope Gregory, with his famous 'Not Angles, but angels' and his instigation of the mission of St Augustine to Kent, shows clearly the courageous spirit of many in this age.

But in the seventh century the promise of new conquests as well as of recovery of lost ground received a terrible shock, for the area previously governed by the Roman Empire had to endure two new waves of invasion. This was the period at which the Arabs burst into Palestine, Syria, Mesopotamia, Persia, Egypt, North Africa and Spain, and at the same time Slavs, Avars and Bulgars broke into Greece and the Balkans. It is one of the miracles of history that Constantinople managed to survive the storm and to remain an outpost of Christendom, holding off further attacks for another eight hundred years, but she was so exhausted in the process and so deeply involved in a desperate struggle for survival that revival, when it came as it did in the eighth century, came from an entirely new quarter. Now was seen the fruit of that baptism of the king of the Franks three hundred years earlier and the steady, persistent preaching of the gospel which had been going on almost unnoticed ever since. Charlemagne, Emperor of the Franks, emerged as the new champion of Christendom, and was crowned by the pope in St Peter's on Christmas Day, in the year 800.

Germany was soon to follow France into the Christian camp, and the ninth century saw further advances. But there were also more invasions. Scandinavian conquerors appeared in Britain, Normandy and Western Russia. Magyars settled in Hungary. Moslems pushed into Sicily, South Italy, and

Greece. The infant church in China was persecuted out of existence. It is hardly surprising that in these terribly unsettled and dangerous times the Church had little or no chance to build up real strength. Decay set in among the monastic orders—their houses were often plundered by invaders. Bishops became secularized, almost hopelessly involved in the fighting and politics of the day. The Papacy was in a terribly insecure position between the Lombards in North Italy and the Moslems in the South, and no great man emerged to lead the Church. Constantinople continued to be in a most precarious situation and was further weakened by internal theological controversy. Only in England, central Europe and the Balkans and, farther afield, in India, were there any signs that Christianity had much life in her. No one could foresee that the foundation of the monastic house of Cluny in the year 910 was, in fact, the beginning of a new lease of life. In general, the position of the Church was further weakened in the face of all her enemies by the fact that the unity of Christendom had been broken, and it is necessary now to survey the history of three almost separate sections: Byzantine, Eastern, and Western.

BYZANTINE CHRISTIANITY

Justinian, who reigned in the years 527 to 565, achieved, as we have seen, an astonishing restoration of the fortunes of the Roman Empire. The recovery was symbolized by the Church in the building, in the year 537, of the great church of St Sophia in Constantinople (Byzantium). But any hopes the emperor had of reuniting the fragments of the empire were to a great extent frustrated by the continuation of the theological dispute of the fifth century. The Christians in the countries on the Eastern border of the old empire had not accepted the decisions of the Council of Chalcedon, and the attempt of Justinian to come to terms with these Monophysite Christians (so called because they maintained that there was only one nature in the person of Christ) were resented in the West as a betrayal of the agreed formula of Chalcedon. A Council called at Constantinople in 553 in an attempt to bring the whole Church together on the basis of a new interpretation of the decisions of Chalcedon satisfied neither the West nor the Monophysites, and the latter continued to spread their views in the East and obtained domination in Antioch and Alexandria. For his part, Justinian had a grievance against the West in that it seemed to prefer a policy of coming to terms with the new rulers there rather than that of joining him in the attempt to unite the old empire under his leadership. In some ways this was a disaster, as Justinian, especially in his legislation, showed himself an outstanding ruler, but there was a danger that the emperor would come to exercise too much influence in church affairs—in fact what is known as Caesaropapalism developed in Byzantium—and the refusal of the West to agree to his policy secured in the end a greater independence for the Church.

The theological question was taken up again at a further Council of Constantinople in the year 680, but this served only to increase the tension between East and West, and any hopes of consolidating the East were, of course, ended by the advance of Islam. This flood left only a few Christian islands in a surrounding sea of Mohammedanism, and it led to an arrest of further development in Constantinople. The last great theologian of the East was John of Damascus who summed up what is now known as Orthodox theology in the eighth century and is regarded as the last creative thinker of the Byzantine Church.

In the eighth and ninth centuries the Eastern Orthodox Church was torn by the Iconoclastic Controversy over the use of images in churches, but the dispute was also over the relations between Church and State and, because both sides in the dispute appealed to the West for support, only served further to embitter the relations between East and West. From these and other shocks of the period many in the Church turned to a purely contemplative monasticism, but heresy also continued to affect the situation and the general impression of this section of the Church at the end of this period is one of weakness.

On the other hand, the end of the period also saw the relaxing of Arab strength and pressure, and Constantinople had managed to survive as the bulwark of Christendom. Slowly, too, the task of converting the Slavs, Moravians, Bulgars, Serbs and Caucasians was undertaken. The Byzantines prided themselves on having maintained the theology, liturgy and the link between Church and State of the Christian Empire, and continued to insist that they rather than the West preserved the tradition of the early Church. So the impression of weakness is not entirely justified, and but for further disputes the Orthodox Church might not have seemed so spent a force.

Disputes continued, however, in particular a struggle for the patriarchate between Ignatius and Photius, which led to schism and brought up once again the question of Caesaropapalism. Yet again the West became involved in the struggle, and new issues caused further drifting apart of East and West. Rival claims for supremacy in church affairs in Bulgaria and in the Mediterranean area in general caused difficulties, and the final straw was a fresh theological dispute. The West had inserted in the Creed a phrase declaring that the Holy Spirit proceeded from the Father *and the Son*, defending it on the grounds that it merely made explicit what had hitherto been implicit. But the Eastern Orthodox Church insisted that this was tampering with the traditional creed of Christendom, and took its stand on its orthodoxy in contrast with the new-fangled unorthodoxy of the West. On this question all attempts to reunite East and West were to founder.

CHURCHES OF THE EAST

In the meantime, while the difficulties between East and West were increasing, other groups of Christians of the farther East had begun to go their own way. Justinian had done what he could to mend the cracks which had appeared, but the situation was, in fact, past mending. The Romans had never succeeded in establishing a really decisive control of the East, and, as the Empire weakened, many of the subject peoples in that area came under other domination or made a bid for independence. Thus national and theological differences often went hand in hand, and it could even be argued that it was patriotic to hold a theological outlook different from that of Constantinople. It was in these circumstances that the Monophysite movement grew in strength after the Council of Chalcedon, and it was not long before it had established control in Egypt, Nubia and Ethiopia. Syria and Armenia were also largely affected, and another version of the same movement, Nestorianism, spread into Persia, central Asia, India and China. The first Nestorian missionaries arrived in China in 635 and maintained their work there until the middle of the ninth century. But a severe persecution began in 845, and when Christian monks arrived in China in 980, they found no trace of the earlier movement.

From the Church's point of view, it was a disaster that this eastern version of Christianity became isolated, and language difficulties did not make the position any easier—part of the problem in the Monophysite controversy was that the ideas of Hellenistic theology could not be easily translated into the less sophisticated languages of the East, and so unnecessary misunderstanding arose. But in the political situation of the time, even if the churches had been agreed in theology, it would have been almost impossible to maintain fellowship, and the situation became even more difficult, of course, with the rise of Islam. The surprising thing is that Christianity of any sort survived in this region, but the Coptic churches of Egypt and Ethiopia which we know today are the direct descendants of the survivors, and we shall note in due course the later history of these and other Christian communities in this area.

THE CHURCH IN THE WEST

While the Church was rapidly losing ground in the original cradle of the Faith, the situation in the West was very different. For all their ferocity, the barbarian invasions in this part of

Europe did not present the same problems as in the East, and, as we have seen, the partially successful resistance of Constantinople to Islam protected the West from the new, rival, militant faith. The barbarians, some of whom had been already in touch with Arian and other missionaries, wishing now to settle in the lands which they had conquered, showed themselves surprisingly willing to listen to Christian preachers and to adopt the religion of the people whom they had conquered. The result was that many of the newcomers turned from Arianism to the Catholic faith, and others were newly converted to what had been the religion of the later Roman Empire. The Church, moreover, was in the West much freer than in the East from imperial control, and in its new-found independence was to prove much more adaptable to the new situation. But it was the growth of western monasticism which contributed as much as anything to the new advance of the Church. The monasteries became centres which retained the best of the old culture and also acted as centres from which missionary activity could be undertaken. The great name is that of Benedict who, in the years 528 to 529, founded the famous monastery of Monte Cassino and established a rule of life for the monks which was to be the basis of all future developments in monastic life. In particular, monks took vows of absolute obedience, poverty and chastity. They held no private property; their clothes, their tools, their writing materials, everything belonged to the community. Every moment of the day was fully organized for them in either worship—the great 'work of God'—or work of a charitable or household nature. Under obedience to their abbot, they were thus men completely at the disposal of the Church, and, although with the growth of the movement the work which they undertook became more varied, sometimes at the price of slackness over spiritual exercises, they provided an invaluable reserve of man-power for the Church in many departments of its life, and the monasteries became training-centres for many of its leaders. More will be said later of their continuing influence.

The Church also took over some of the functions of government—the protection of the poor, for instance—and the popes of Rome began to play a decisive part in the affairs of the West. Gregory I, in particular, pope from 590 to 604, set a standard of able administration and missionary zeal which was to be an inspiration in future years. His counsels to Augustine for the foundation of the English Church were the model for a great deal of missionary activity, with instructions about church finance, the organization of dioceses, the form of liturgy to be used, and, of course, the assumption that this English mission was completely under the direction of Rome. The position of the papacy was further strengthened by the use of such documents as the Donation of Constantine and the Decretals of Isidore, which, although later proved to be forgeries, nevertheless in the interim were genuinely thought to provide a legal basis for the claims of the Church to make her voice heard in the affairs of western Europe.

So the task of converting their conquerors was enthusiastically undertaken by Christian preachers. Italy, Spain and Gaul were gradually won over. The great British missionary, Columban, travelled to France, the Vosges, Milan and Genoa preaching the gospel. The English themselves had been converted in the sixth and seventh centuries by Celtic monks such as Columba and Aidan, working from Iona and Lindisfarne, and by the Roman mission led by Augustine, Wilfrid and Theodore. The Celtic monks, in particular, had a great reputation for sanctity. One of them, Colman, was said to have a cock to wake him for Lauds in the morning, a mouse to nibble his ear or gnaw at his clothes if he overslept, and a fly which marked his place if he was called away from his reading. Another, Cuthbert, was watched one night as he waded into the sea and spent the dark hours praying with the waves up to his arm and neck, while in the morning his feet were dried for him by sea otters. The mutual sympathy between saints and the animal kingdom was, of course, to have another expression later in the life of Francis of Assisi, but by the side of their Celtic contemporaries, the 'Roman' missionaries emerge, for all their courage, as rather humdrum characters, good organizers. The Synod of Whitby in 664 had however, firmly linked the English church to the Catholic Church on the Continent, and from this base, not only Columban in the South, but also Willibrord and Boniface in Germany, Holland and France, in the seventh and eighth centuries, continued the work of spreading the gospel. The English, indeed, played a most important part in the missionary work of this period, but others, too, were at work, and a decisive moment arrived when Charlemagne conquered the Saxons and forced them to accept Christianity, despite the fact that Alcuin, a British scholar who held a position of great influence at the Frankish court, protested at the ruthless use of compulsion for such a purpose. A start was also made on the Scandinavians, and here, as in other cases, whole masses of people, led by their chieftains and kings, came over to Christianity. It cannot be pretended that in all cases the conversion went very deep. One of the later apostles of the North was, for instance, Olaf Tryggvason, a viking pirate, who was baptized in the Scilly Isles and then returned to his home in Norway and offered his countrymen the alternative of conversion or death. The mission of this muscular Christian met with considerable success, though he himself eventually perished by the sword. But even before his appearance, by the end of the eighth century a great part of the north and west was nominally Christian, and the Church was faced with the enormous task of consolidating her position. The missionaries had won her that opportunity.

The importance of the Carolingians needs to be stressed at this point. They had extended their influence through France, Belgium, the Netherlands, Western and Southern Germany, Switzerland, Austria, North Italy, Spain, and even into the Adriatic region. The Franks whom they ruled had, as we have seen, been the first of the barbarian people to turn to Christianity. Now, under Charlemagne, they were clearly the dominant power in Europe, and this meant that the Church had won a powerful ally. The alliance between the Franks and the Papacy was sealed in 800 when the Pope crowned Charlemagne Emperor, and the Church in the West was definitely casting in her lot with a new order. The coronation, in fact, provoked protests from Constantinople which claimed that she had maintained the succession of the Roman Empire, and this was, therefore, another cause of the increasing division between East and West. But so far as the Church in the West was concerned, the new alliance was clearly more advantageous than any attempt to revive the Byzantine Empire. Charlemagne, moreover, showed every sign of a genuine desire to advance the cause of Christianity, not only on the battlefield. His court became a centre of learning, and his great gifts of organization were placed at the service of the Church as well as of the State. New rules were made for the monasteries, regulations were made for priests and their work among their congregations, the worship of the Church was improved and a revision of the liturgy undertaken. So it appeared that the Church was at the beginning of a period of increasing prosperity.

The period is also important in other ways. We have already noted the development along certain lines in theology, though the introduction of the new phrase into the Creed had caused dispute with the East. Gottschalk revived some of the teaching of the great Augustine of Hippo, in particular his doctrine of predestination. The theory of the Mass began to develop along the lines which led in the end to the doctrine of transubstantiation. There was a beginning, too, in the direction of the later medieval practices of private confession and penance. The lines of Roman Catholicism were being laid down. An essential element in this process was, of course, the growth of the power of the Papacy. This has already been noted in passing in reference to the missionary work of the Church, but it developed in other ways too. In the West there was no rival to the see of Rome in its claims of supremacy on the grounds of apostolic foundation. Events in the East had destroyed or weakened the influence of the other ancient centres of authority, and the bishop of Rome towered above all others. The bishop, moreover, had entered into the even more ancient traditions of Roman government, and it seemed that he alone was capable of transmitting to future generations the heritage of the imperial city. In the persons of Gregory I and Nicholas I, Rome produced leaders of exceptional quality, and the popes began to underline claims of primacy which had already been made in an earlier age. It seemed clear that the keys of the kingdom were in the hands of the successors of St Peter, and the coronation of Charlemagne only served to emphasize the authority of the bishop of Rome to supervise the affairs of Christendom. The power of the papacy had by no means reached its peak as yet, but the tendency towards absolute supremacy was already appearing.

Unfortunately, however, the rosy prospects envisaged by the alliance between the Papacy and the Franks did not immediately develop, and the ninth and tenth centuries saw a decline in the fortunes of the Church. In the first place, the power of the Frankish Empire was broken up and the strength of the Church's ally was undermined. Instead of working with an all-powerful Emperor, the Church found itself faced with the growing power of feudalism, so that at all levels, Pope, bishops, priests, found their claims to the right of government being challenged by secular lords who also claimed absolute obedience from their subjects and tenants. Europe was thrown into confusion once again by the Scandinavian invasions, and in the time of chaos it happened that there was no decisive leadership from Rome.

But all was not lost. As at an earlier period, England once again provided leadership which was to bring a new order out of chaos. Under king Alfred and bishop Dunstan the Danes were first held and then converted, and the English Church began to show the way forward. In 910 a new monastery was founded at Cluny in France, and this foundation was to prove the beginning not only of a revival of monasticism, but also of a revival of leadership in the Church as a whole. Once the Scandinavian invasions had spent their force, it was possible to institute movements of reform in the Church, and the

D

Western Church began to emerge in new strength. Its characteristics were that it was Latin rather than Greek—in contrast with the Eastern Orthodox Church—it was freer of State control than its eastern counterpart; it was based on the authority of Rome; monasticism was to play an increasingly influential part; it came to terms with feudalism and found its place in feudal society; and, in the matter of theology, Augustine became the dominant voice. Indeed, it began to appear that the city of God (the title of the book which Augustine had written at the time of the collapse of the Roman Empire) might after all be founded on earth, though the medieval church was to transform the ideas of Augustine to some extent in the days that followed.

CHAPTER THREE

The Middle Ages, A.D. 950-1350

THE CHURCH in the Middle Ages found itself in a very different situation from that of the previous five hundred years. Those years had been marked by a tremendous shifting of the world's population which had brought an enormous number of invasions into Europe and the Mediterranean basin and with them all manner of chaos and confusion. By a miracle, as it seemed, Christianity had survived the crisis, and now, in the years of comparative stability which followed, the Church responded by resuming its advance. In the hundred years from 950 onwards such an expansion of Christianity was achieved as has only been exceeded in the modern period after 1500, and far exceeded anything that had been achieved previously. One of the most encouraging features of this advance was the ability Christendom showed in making some slight impression upon lands which had succumbed to Islam.

ADVANCE

English missionaries were once again to the fore in the Scandinavian countries. This was a natural consequence of the conversion of the Danes who had settled in England, a reminder of the fact that the new movement had actually been set in motion before 950, but in the new period the success continued and eventually spread as far as Iceland and Greenland in one direction, and Kiev in another. Earlier beginnings in central Europe and the Balkans were also extended by the conversion of the Slav countries of Czecho-Slovakia (where Good King Wenceslaus symbolized the new triumphs of the Church), Poland and Hungary. In the South, Spain and Sicily were recaptured from Islam. In Mesopotamia

an Arab tribe was won, though some of the islands of Christianity which had hitherto survived in the Mohammedan areas
suffered some decline in this same period. Work in North-
west Europe, which had appeared so promising in the
Carolingian era, was resumed and consolidated. In central
Asia the Keraits adopted Nestorianism, as did several other
tribes, and for a time the Mongol conquerors of this part of the
world seemed friendly to Christianity in its various forms. It
was not long before Franciscan and Dominican missionaries
were penetrating as far as India and China. Raymond Lull, a
Franciscan, is perhaps the outstanding name of the thirteenth
and fourteenth centuries. He founded a school in Majorca for
the study of Arabic and Chaldean, and was eventually to give
his life on the mission field, being stoned to death in Tunis
by the Saracens in 1315. But the travels of the friars in all
directions were astonishing. Quite apart from their work in
Europe, we find them in such distant places as Morocco,
Libya, Tunis and Algiers, the Holy Land and Egypt, Cape
Verde, Guinea and the Congo, Persia, Sumatra, Java, Borneo
and Tibet. Work in such far away and dangerous places,
carrying the fight into enemy strongholds, was not achieved
without many martyrdoms, and not all of the work was of
lasting consequence, but the missionary attempts of the
medieval church are much more considerable than is often
realized.

Side by side with this preaching of the gospel went another
attempt at advance, but one so mixed in its motives that it
ended eventually in disaster. This was the series of Crusades.
On their spiritual side, they were largely inspired by Bernard
of Clairvaux, and were a genuine, if misguided, project to
recover the lands lost to Islam. They could also be used in
other areas and against heretics. But the crusaders became so
involved in national and commercial rivalries that the original
purpose was lost, and the crowning folly came when the
fourth crusade turned aside from its declared object in order
to attack Constantinople and establish a Latin kingdom there
which lasted for fifty years. The disastrous effect of this on the

relations between East and West can be easily imagined, and in the end, despite all the heroism and faith, nothing of enduring value came from these extraordinary experiments in militant Christianity. The military orders that were founded had eventually to be suppressed, though for a time they contributed something to the idea of chivalry, the protection of travellers and the poor, and the needs of commerce. The Papacy, too, though for a time it won great prestige from its encouragement of the crusades, in the end gained nothing from them, and must bear some of the responsibility for their later degeneration and failure. The temptation to use the crusades for merely political ends was apparently irresistible.

But, taking the period as a whole, and weighing the successes against the failures, it must be said that the medieval idea of using Christendom as a centre from which the light of the gospel might be spread all round the world, was, at its best, a notable conception so soon after the Dark Ages.

THE CHURCH IN THE WEST

Quite as important as the missionary activity of the Church in this period was the work of consolidation and reform that was necessary in areas where Christianity had already taken root in earlier years. As we have noted, much of the early work of conversion had been in the nature of mass movements and was in consequence very superficial. A good deal of superstition still remained, and many pagan customs had merely been given a veneer of Christianity. A concerted effort was necessary to make their faith more real to ordinary people and, it may be added, to many of the leaders in Church and State as well.

In this process the various monastic orders played a decisive part, and throughout this period there was a succession of reforms and creation of new orders, which set entirely new standards for the life of the Church though basically they were all founded on the old Benedictine Rule. In this respect the foundation of Cluny in 910 was of immense influence, and it is possible to trace a great deal of the reform that gradually mounted to the Cluniac movement. But other orders also were added, the Cistercians, for instance, who owed much of their importance to the tremendous reputation of Bernard of Clairvaux, and the Carthusians with their very rigorous standards of discipline. Some cathedrals also became staffed by canons regular, who, although not monks in the strict sense of the word, yet had their lives organized by rule very similar to that of the monasteries. The effect of the monastic movement was felt once again at all levels of church life. Not only did it set high standards of personal devotion, but it also gave much attention to scholarship and learning. It produced missionaries and leaders of all kinds—many of the men who took the lead as reforming bishops were trained in monasteries. It increased the social and charitable work of the Church through care of the poor, hospitals and schools. But above all it provided the reformers in the Church with a body of agents for their policy. The monks, unlike parish priests, were independent of lay lords and bishops, though bishops were always trying to assert their authority. The monk owed obedience to the head of his house, through him to the head of his order, and through him to the Pope. The basic vows of the monk were those of poverty, chastity and obedience— obedience, perhaps, above all—and, though it was possible for this agency to be abused, nevertheless in the great days of monasticism here was the tool which the reformers needed to raise the standard of the Church's life.

The enthusiasm which went into the monastic movement, especially in the eleventh and twelfth centuries, was in the thirteenth directed into fresh channels. The coming of the Friars brought tremendous impetus, not only to missionary work, as we have seen, but also to the life of the Church at large. Essentially a preaching movement originally directed against ignorance and heresy, the Franciscans, Dominicans, Carmelites, Augustinians and others, were soon making great contributions in education and social service also, and the life of Francis has, of course, remained an inspiration to the Church for all time. He brought to Christianity not only a spirit of self-denial, giving up the wealth and position of a prosperous merchant's son in order to comfort lepers and other outcasts, but also one of simplicity and gaiety which refreshed the whole Church. '*Joculatores Domini*', God's merry men, he and his companions were called. Like the monk, the friar took vows of poverty, chastity and obedience, but unlike the monk he had, in general, a more roving commission, and once again, since he was not subject to local authority, he proved an ideal agent of reform. The friars rapidly achieved great popularity and this brought a considerable amount of jealousy from the older orders and from parish and episcopal authorities so that, in the end, the free-lancing of the movement had to be controlled to some extent by licence. By this time the friars had turned some of their energies towards education and they were to play a leading part in the building up of the great universities of the Middle Ages. Men like Roger Bacon, a pioneer in many ways of modern scientific enquiry, owed their education to the friars, and, though in university circles their claims to independence aroused as much rivalry as their other activities elsewhere, the friars were as effective as the monks had been at an earlier age in producing leaders for the various affairs of Church and State.

Side by side with these two great religious movements, the popular religious movements of the time must be noted. The third orders, as some were called, singing guilds, flagellants and *beguines*, and many others, represented the layman's response to the fervour of the times. At their best they indicated an increasing tendency on the part of ordinary folk to take their religion more seriously. But unfortunately in many cases they degenerated into extravagance and heresy. They were largely ascetic in character, but tended to revolt against authority and to become anti-sacramental. The two most notable examples are those of the Waldensians and the Cathari, and against them the organized Church felt justified in launching not only the friars, but also the Crusades and the Inquisition. It was essential, so the authorities felt, to save people at all costs from extravagance and error, but the popular movements indicated that there were expressions of religious life which were not yet catered for by the Church, and it is perhaps in these movements that we should look for the beginning of those feelings which were eventually to find their outlet in the Reformation.

But meanwhile tremendous efforts had been made by the Church in the way of reform. It must be remembered that, although the invasions had ceased, a dreadful legacy of unrest and disturbance had been left, and a great part of the history of the times is concerned with the attempts of the rulers of both State and Church to establish authority and a respect for law and order. Sometimes this led to clashes between Church and State as they disputed the boundaries of authority, but, when kings and bishops worked together, considerable progress was made. The work of Alfred and Dunstan in England has already been mentioned. In Germany there was similar co-operation between the rulers and men like Bernard of Hildesheim. But most important of all was the work of German kings which led to the creation of the Holy Roman Empire and the reform of the Papacy. As the Papacy itself was reformed and grew in strength, a new spirit of direction and authority came into all church affairs. In 1049 the importance of the cardinals at Rome was increased, and in 1059 the cardinals were given complete control of papal elections. A succession of Popes like Nicholas II and Alexander II and of cardinals like Humbert and Hildebrand (who himself became Pope as Gregory VII) stepped up the discipline and standards of the Church in all departments of its life, and the Church gradually increased in zeal and influence.

There were dangers in the claims which the Church was making of supremacy in the affairs of Christendom, but in part the movement for reform and authority was a movement for independence. If the leaders of the Church had not taken the stand they did, the alternative would have been to succumb to the equally extravagant claims to absolute power which were being made by emperors and kings. This explains the bitterness of such struggles as those between Pope Gregory VII and Emperor Henry IV, and between Anselm and Thomas à Becket and the kings of England. 'England is not a bush', said Henry II during his struggle with Becket, 'that can hold two such robins as the archbishop and myself.' Much could be said on both sides, but the question of ultimate loyalty involved in the Investiture struggle and the dispute over the jurisdiction of ecclesiastical courts were of vital importance. Kings striving to establish the law of the realm could not afford to permit an independent jurisdiction or to recognize as independent some of their leading citizens and land-owners. The Church, on the other hand, could not allow laymen to have the final word in Church affairs. An uneasy compromise was reached, but only when the Church proved herself capable of good government and order, and it was for this reason that the Hildebrandine and other reforms were so important. The movement for reform culminated eventually in the work of Pope Innocent III and the Fourth Lateran Council of 1215, which laid down, among other things, the principle of yearly confession. The decrees of the Lateran Council were widely enforced throughout the Church, and it appeared that the Popes had established their claim of the supremacy of spiritual authority over all secular power. But unfortunately the triumph of the Papacy was followed by decline, and the Church found itself having to adjust its policies to a rising spirit of nationalism. This was symbolized by the Babylonish Captivity of 1309 to 1377 when the Pope resided at Avignon and found himself almost completely in the power of the kings of France.

In realms other than the political, other developments took place in this period. The Church had the monopoly of education, and this was a time of considerable development in schools and universities. This in itself was one reason for the successes of the Church, for rulers seeking educated men to be their ministers had to turn to those who had been educated by the Church. Often this led to men trying to serve two masters, and sometimes churchmen became so involved in affairs of

State that they had little time left for church duties. The abuses to which this gave rise must be left till later. Meanwhile it must be noted that the Church's control of education produced at the highest level great intellectual achievements. In the schools and universities there was a great outburst of creative thought, and the scholasticism of the Church resulted in the elevation of theology to the position of 'the queen of the sciences'. Great debates took place on the relation between faith and reason, on the nature of reality and on the work of Christ, and some of the greatest names in Christian theology: Anselm, Abelard, Bernard of Clairvaux, Peter Lombard, Thomas Aquinas and William of Occam, belong to this period. Unfortunately the steam of creative thought was tending to dry up by the end of the period, and authority took the place of reason as the final justification of Christian faith, so that in later years the Church found herself ill-equipped to deal with new questions raised at the time of the Renaissance and the Reformation. But at its best, in the work of Thomas Aquinas, for instance, scholasticism had made a brave attempt to comprehend all truth within the framework of the Christian Faith and to find some means of reconciling the paths of reason and revelation. This attempt had contributed very largely to the domination which the Church had come to exercise over the whole of the life of Christendom for a brief period.

But this domination was due not only to the intellectuals, it was also built partly on the work of the practical administrators and reformers, who owed much to the guidance of Rome. At the height of her power the Roman Catholic Church seemed to be ready to provide for all the needs of man from the cradle to the grave—and beyond. It is true that the faith of the common man in the Middle Ages was brought to centre on the cross of Christ and all its benefits, but those benefits tended to be more and more controlled and mediated only by the Church. The Church was thoroughly organized on diocesan and parish lines. This was an age of much church building, and as the cathedral and church rose to dominate town and village, so the bishop and priest gained more and more influence over men's lives. The two sacraments of our Lord were added to until there were seven sacraments of the Church: baptism, confirmation, penance, the Mass, ordination, matrimony and extreme unction. Death was an event which could be met only with the help of the Church, and much care was given to funerals. Indulgences began to be introduced and masses for the dead. The help of the saints and of the blessed virgin Mary was sought for this life and the next. Various festivals of the Church were increasingly celebrated, and miracle plays, paintings and stained glass in the churches, drove home the lesson of what was expected of the Christian in this life and what might be his fate in the next if he was disobedient. Christian poetry helped to popularize the teaching of the Faith, and books were produced for the laity as well as for the clergy to instruct them in all the duties of the Christian life. Charitable enterprises on the part of laymen were encouraged, as were pilgrimages and going on crusade. All this, in addition to the normal dues paid for the upkeep of the Church, was thought to be a means of securing salvation. Another means was to cultivate the way of the mystic, though this was only possible for rare souls. But mystics like Richard Rolle, who had been greatly influenced by the Franciscans, had great influence in their turn on account of their holiness, and because their example tended to encourage others in the knowledge of the love of God. So, in these and other ways, the Church sought to secure the safety of the Christian soul, and if a man suffered the terrible penalty of excommunication, his case was considered to be hopeless because he no longer benefited from the ministrations of the Church. Under this threat, even kings and emperors bowed to the wishes of the rulers of the Church. In 1077, for instance, the Emperor Henry IV waited as a penitent for four days in the snow outside the papal residence at Canossa until Pope Gregory VII removed the sentence which he had pronounced on him. Many of the claims which the Church made seem now to be inexcusable, but when we come to consider the protests that were made against the abuses of the Church, it is well to remember that there were men like Chaucer's poor parson, teaching 'Christ's Lore', but following it first himself.

In the wider life of Christendom as a whole, the Church also made her voice heard. She set the standards of morals and art, and even of science. She tried to restrain tyranny by advancing the theory of the just war, and to restrain the bloodthirstiness of the times by insisting on peaces and truces of God. She sought to bring some sort of honourable conduct into commercial affairs by insisting on the just price against usury. And always she was at hand for the protection of the poor and sick and aged. Among the many foundations of all types in this period, the famous St Bartholomew's hospital was, for instance, founded in the twelfth century by Rahere in Smithfield, London. It is only right to remember, especially in view of abuses and criticisms of the medieval Church that later arose, that, for all the romantic colour that has often been given to them, the Middle Ages were in fact rough and brutal in many ways. That in these conditions the Church was able, with all her faults, to be so strong a force for civilization, was no mean achievement.

EASTERN CHURCHES

The story of the other churches outside the great drama of the West is of a very different kind.

After her heroic resistance to and recovery from invasion in the Dark Ages, Byzantium was slowly collapsing. In the eleventh century the Turks established themselves so securely in Asia Minor that this territory was never recaptured, and at the same time the coming of Normans to Southern Italy and Greece brought to an end Byzantine influence in areas which she had previously claimed to be within her sphere. Then there came the tragedy of the Fourth Crusade in 1204. The attack against Constantinople was occasioned largely by the commercial rivalry of Venice and Genoa, but, although there was some recovery after the collapse of the Latin kingdom after some fifty years, the whole ground was never regained.

So fellow Christians as much as Moslem Turks were in the final issue responsible for the fall of Constantinople.

In the circumstances the loss of strength and the conservatism of the Byzantine Church are not surprising, but it must not be thought that the cause was entirely lost in this area. Occasionally the Patriarch showed surprising zeal for independence, and, although the danger of Caesaropapalism continued, the Church was never completely submerged. Monasticism in the East also continued to have considerable influence, though it was by no means so missionary minded as its Western counterpart, and there were some developments in mysticism parallel to those in the West. But the most serious fact of these times was the continually widening rift between the East and West, and for this, obstinacy and pride on both sides must be blamed. These Christians did not love one another, and, when they might have co-operated to their mutual advantage, they fell at each others throats. A hundred and fifty years before the Fourth Crusade, Rome had actually brought matters to a head by excommunicating the Church of Constantinople. This was probably intended as a threat rather than as a final judgement, but, despite continued negotiations in succeeding years, the two churches remained in fact cut off from communion with one another. The Roman Church, moreover, in pursuance of its claims to supremacy, sent missionaries into areas owning allegiance to Constantinople. The result of this policy was the creation of what came to be known as Uniate churches, owning allegiance to Rome but continuing the practice and liturgy of Eastern Orthodoxy.

Despite growing weakness and despite Roman rivalry, the Byzantine Church, however, managed to win some successes. Her history continued to be most chequered, but preachers in Bulgaria, Serbia and Russia laid foundations for the future, so that when the city of Constantine eventually fell, the leadership of Eastern Orthodoxy passed to new lands.

In the meantime, the fate of the Monophysites in Egypt, Nubia and Ethiopia was even more serious. Here Islam made increasing gains which resulted in the deterioration of these struggling Christian communities. In face of bitter persecution the Coptic churches became much weaker and fell prey to internal corruption. But still a small minority survived to carry on the traditions of these people right into modern times.

In Armenia, which had been the first nation to call itself entirely Christian, this period saw at first some signs of strength. The Armenians extended their influence into Cilicia, and, during the period of the Crusades, there was some contact between this country and Rome and the West. When the Crusades petered out, however, this contact was not maintained, and, though there is some evidence of continued life in the Church through its literature, hymns and prayers, the Armenian Church had no decisive part to play in the history of the Church as a whole.

Farther East in areas where Nestorianism had become established, the period was one of considerable development. In fact, at the end of the period Nestorianism was more widespread and prosperous than it had ever been before. Its influence may be gathered from the number of its rulers—a Patriarch, with twenty-five metropolitans and between two hundred and two hundred and fifty bishops. As at an earlier period, it seems that the Nestorians profited from the favour of the Mongol rulers of the time, who used the Christian minority in these areas to offset possible nationalistic movements against their imperialist policy. There is also clear evidence in this period from Western travellers of the existence of Christian communities in India, and once again we remember the travels of the Friars.

But on the whole the situation of Christianity in the East was very precarious. The Byzantine power was, as we have seen, on the wane. In Asia and Africa Christian minorities were yielding ground to Islam, and there were no real signs of fresh vitality. The Church was to suffer great losses in this area in the years after 1350.

CHAPTER FOUR

The Twilight of the Middle Ages, A.D. 1350-1500

THE STORY of the Middle Ages has not been, as we have seen, one of universal success for the Church. But, when we consider the brighter side of the story in the West and remember the heroic resistance against odds in the East, it is startling to discover how serious was the collapse of Christendom in the late fourteenth and fifteenth centuries. Almost without warning the Church found itself once again faced with great and terrible crisis, and it was not unreasonable to suppose that Christianity was becoming a declining force in world affairs.

CHRISTIANITY IN THE EAST

In the far East the decisive event was the collapse of the great Mongol Empire. For political motives the Mongol rulers had been not unfavourable to Christian enterprise, but with their disappearance the second attempt to establish Christianity in China came to an abrupt end, and Nestorianism was almost entirely obliterated in central Asia. The period was one of advance for both Buddhism and Mohammedanism, and the Monophysites as well as the Nestorians suffered great losses. The few scattered communities that survived were disunited and unable to help one another, and the result of the political and religious changes was that to this day large areas of Asia and Africa remain to be evangelized afresh.

The Coptic churches of Egypt and Ethiopia (or Abyssinia as it is called in modern times) suffered further shrinkage, and the Church in Nubia was on the point of disappearance altogether.

In Armenia the Christian forces were divided by the establishment of a considerable number of Uniate churches, but, despite its divided allegiance, Christian witness was maintained in this area.

Farther west there came a fresh outburst of Turkish power, and the Turks established themselves in the Balkans. In 1453, the great bastion of Christianity, Constantinople, which had held out for so long against all enemies, at last fell, and the church of St Sophia was turned into a mosque. Asia Minor, the scene of so much of Paul's missionary work and of the early triumphs of the Church, became largely Moslem, but here and there within the new Turkish Empire Christianity survived under great pressure and became identified as the inspiration of nationalistic movements against Turkish imperialism. The Turks, in fact, did not always attempt to stamp out Christianity altogether, preferring to recognize and use Christian communities for military and taxation purposes, so that the Eastern Orthodox Church was not entirely obliterated. In Constantinople itself, for instance, this was the period of the Phanariots and Janissaries, Christians who managed to come to some sort of terms with their overlords and by compromise to maintain something of a continuing Christian community.

The one great area of development was Russia, where monks were again to the fore in missionary, educational and charitable activity. Unfortunately, a quarrel developed between two groups, one following the more practical activities of the monastic life and the other, the minority led by Nilus, turning to the hermit life, to extreme asceticism and to mysticism. The situation was further complicated by heresies, and two main types emerged: the Judaizers and the Strigolniks, who were chiefly notable for their anti-clericalism. But on the whole, the developments in Russia represented an important recovery of Eastern Orthodoxy, and the Patriarch of Moscow usurped the place of the Patriarch of Constantinople as leader of this branch of the Church in the years to come.

The fall of Constantinople brought to an end, of course, the long and bitter rivalry with Rome. The Roman Church continued its policy of seeking to win the Christians of the

East to an acceptance of its authority, and this means of establishing the unity of the Church seemed at last to be meeting with some success when a considerable number of Eastern bishops accepted the invitation to join in the Council of Ferrara and Florence in the years 1438 and 1439. But, though a few of these bishops did in fact accept the supremacy of Rome, in the end the majority of the Eastern Orthodox Church rejected this new advance on Rome's part, and their Church continued its independent existence.

CHRISTIANITY IN THE WEST

The decline of the Church in the West was due, not to attacks from outside, but rather to the political situation in Christendom itself and to inner decay. The most serious cause of this was the decline of the Papacy. The Babylonish Captivity was followed by the Great Schism of 1378 to 1417, during which, at one time, three men were being supported by rival parties in their separate claims to be regarded as the true successor of Peter, bishop of Rome. It was not surprising that men like the monk of Malmesbury should pray: 'Lord Jesus! either take away the pope from our midst or lessen the power which he presumes to have over our people!' And such extreme epithets as 'a poisonous weed', 'head vicar of the fiend', and 'a simple idiot who might be a damned devil in hell', though exaggerated and hardly charitable, showed in what contempt some Christians held the titular head of the Church. The chaotic situation eventually led to a demand for a Council, and the Council of Constance of 1414 to 1418, after much negotiation and intrigue, finally resulted in the emergence of Martin V as the universally acknowledged Pope and in the reiteration of the doctrine of papal supremacy. This was not the result which the advocates of the Conciliar Movement had really been working for. It had been suggested that the only way to guarantee the integrity of the Church was to insist that the authority of the Pope himself depended on the authority of the whole Church represented by its bishops meeting in council. But the reformers were defeated, and the

E

moral decline of the papacy continued until the situation was reached that a Borgia was on the papal throne (Alexander VI, from 1492 to 1503), while his son Cesare sought to carve out for himself in Italy a petty princedom. To see the papal family thus enthusiastically involved in Italian politics and cynically disregarding the Church's insistence on clerical celibacy—Alexander was, of course, unmarried—was to bring the highest position in the Christian Church into the utmost contempt.

Side by side with the decline of the Papacy went the decline of the Holy Roman Empire and the feudal system with which the Church had come to terms and been identified. The rise of new kingdoms breaking up the old unity of Empire was only possible after protracted struggles like the Wars of the Roses, which resulted in one noble family rising supreme over all others and establishing a strong central monarchy. When this happened, one of the inevitable consequences was that kings began to curtail papal privileges within their kingdoms on the ground that these privileges represented interference in affairs of State by a foreign power, and it must be admitted that papal politics often lent colour to this charge. But in so far as this meant a severe restriction of papal resources and influence, it was a serious setback for the Church. In earlier days it had been thought possible to divide empire between spiritual and temporal powers, and to compare them with the sun and moon in their different spheres, but the highest point of papal theory had been stated in the Bull *Unam Sanctam* by Pope Boniface VIII as recently as 1302. According to him, the Church had been granted the swords of both spiritual and temporal power and every human creature—even the mightiest prince—was, therefore, subject to the Pope. It was clear that the new national rulers were not going to accept dogma of this order, and the Papacy had to bow to the new forces that were in being. Bishops in the new kingdoms found themselves similarly facing a new situation. Within the feudal system the ecclesiastical lords had been as important as the lay lords, and, because through their holding of church property they had also been leading landlords, a careful series of adjustments had been necessary in order to safeguard the independence of the Church. Since, in these adjustments the bishops had leant heavily on the authority of the Pope, now that the power of the Papacy had declined, fresh measures had to be sought to secure the independence of the Church for the future, and in the meantime it often appeared that bishops could only do what kings allowed.

Another factor not to be forgotten in the history of the later Middle Ages is the tragic effects of the plague known as the Black Death which ravaged the whole of Europe about the middle of the fourteenth century. It is estimated that in Northern Europe the plague carried away a third of the entire population, and in England as much as a half. It was especially virulent in places where men lived close together, and in consequence monasteries and other clergy houses were very seriously affected. Other clergy were exposed, too, to the worst effects of the plague in the course of their ministrations to the sick, especially among the poor who also suffered terribly. The result of this was a serious reduction of clerical man-power, which was one of the contributing causes to the corruption of the clergy at this time. Such evils as absenteeism, pluralism and simony often occurred simply because there were no longer enough clergy to carry out all the duties of the Church, and there followed a grave deterioration in the training and in the quality of the clergy.

In addition to this the orders of monks and friars had lost a great deal of their original inspiration. The high principle of evangelical poverty had been turned by some men into what was almost a vested interest. Bonaventura, himself a Franciscan, had said: 'The sight of a begging friar in the distance was more formidable than a robber.' The orders, largely through benefactions, had become owners of large properties, and so much time had to be given to the administration of affairs that there was often little clear difference between an ecclesiastical and a lay landlord. Churchmen became to a large extent indistinguishable from other country gentlemen. More time for business meant less time for prayer and preaching. And the growth of schools and universities outside the monasteries and other clergy houses meant less time given to study inside them. Even some of the charitable work formerly done by church institutions was now passing into the hands of guilds and other organizations. The pattern of medieval life was clearly undergoing great changes, and it must be confessed that the Church hardly kept up with the times.

In the intellectual sphere, too, the Church was losing her grip. Her former monopoly of education had gone and there had come into being a group of educated laymen able to rival the churchmen on their own ground. Rulers no longer had to rely on the Church for a supply of educated servants, and this was particularly so in the realm of law where the Church courts found themselves increasingly challenged by the king's courts and the law of the land. Scholasticism had now passed its peak, and the old ways of thought fostered by the Church were being examined by scholars brought up in the new traditions of the Renaissance. This new learning was not necessarily anti-Christian, but often it was, as is seen by the works of such men as Boccaccio and Machiavelli, and when it was it was accompanied by new standards of morals in statecraft, art and life in general.

But all was not lost, and there was still much to be set on the credit side of the Church's life. The Church could still produce saints like Joan of Arc and Catherine of Siena. She could still produce mystics like Lady Julian of Norwich and works of devotion such as the *Theologica Germanica*. The Brothers and Sisters of the Common Life and the Congregation of Windesheim still bore witness to a zeal for the devotional life, and this was the period of Thomas à Kempis and his *Imitation of Christ*. Women began to play an increasing part in religious life. There was considerable stress on the necessity of preaching. Devotion centred on the Stations of the Cross. Hymns and drama and art continued to be pressed into the service of the Church. There were some attempts at monastic reform, and even the use of the Inquisition, especially in Spain, might be said to show a real, though misguided, zeal for the Faith.

The work of Christian humanists became of great importance, bridging the gap between this age and the age to follow, showing that the new learning could be put to Christian use. Sir Thomas More, scholar, statesman and churchman, tried to preserve the best of the old world in the new, and was to give his life in resisting the dubious policy of Henry VIII. Dean Colet of St Paul's with his lectures on the Epistle to the Romans was to set new standards of scholarship and preaching. Erasmus, with his new edition of the Greek Testament, was to stimulate fresh discussion of the Bible which bore fruit in many Reformation centres, and his work was not intended for scholars only: 'I wish that even the weakest woman might read the Gospels and the Epistles of St Paul. I wish that they were translated into all languages, so as to be read and understood not only by Scots and Irishmen, but even by Saracens and Turks. I long for the day when the husbandman shall sing portions of them to himself as he follows the plough, when the weaver shall hum them to the tune of his spindle, when the traveller shall wile away with their stories the weariness of his journey.'

Before and behind these men there had been John Wyclif and John Hus, in England and Bohemia respectively, who had shown that at an even earlier period the conscience of the Church could not be stifled. The work of Wyclif in criticizing without fear or favour the abuses of the medieval Church, in translating the Bible into the language of the people, and in sending out his 'poor preachers', the Lollards, to call his fellow-countrymen back to true religion, was of immense importance. The work of Hus was of a similar order, and, although he was condemned by the Council of Constance—as were the teachings of Wyclif—and although no direct connection can be established between these men and the later reformers, the work of such men undoubtedly had a considerable effect, and from their day onward the leaven was working secretly towards a reformation. In Italy itself, the very stronghold of papal power, Savonarola did not hesitate to criticize the infamous Alexander VI. The leaders of the Church at all levels might be failing in their responsibilities, it might be said that on the whole the morals of the clergy were worse than those of their lay contemporaries, but still there were men thrown up by the Church who criticized not only on the grounds of dubious policy, but also out of a true concern for real religion. And when the time came for the decisive word to be spoken, there were thousands of common folk who were ready to respond and even to lay down their lives for the truth.

CHAPTER FIVE

The Modern Church, A.D. 1500-1960

THE STORY of the modern Church is on a much vaster scale than anything that has gone before. The scene is no longer merely the Mediterranean lands—with a few noises off —but the whole world. We shall deal with it in five sections: the Reformation and its consequences; the Counter-Reformation and the development of Roman Catholicism; the later history of the Eastern Orthodox Church; the expansion of the Church; and the Ecumenical Movement.

THE REFORMATION AND ITS CONSEQUENCES

The great influence of Martin Luther was due to the fact, not so much that he was an original thinker, as that in him the growing criticism of the Church of the Middle Ages found its champion and representative. His own criticism of the Church began, not with a wholesale onslaught, but with an attack upon the sale of Indulgences by which the Pope promised, in return for what degenerated only too easily into a mere cash transaction, to secure remission of some of the penalties of the sin of the purchasers. But once the battle was joined, the argument moved irresistibly on until Luther was taking a view of religion quite at variance with the old, and the Protestant position emerged. In 1519, two years after the publication of his Ninety-five Theses, he asserted that the Bible and not the Pope was the ultimate authority for Christians, and that men were saved by faith alone. In 1520 he published a series of tracts which established the doctrine of the priesthood of all believers. In the same year he was excommunicated, but burnt a copy of the bull of excommunication in public. In 1521 he translated the New Testament into German. By 1530 the full Lutheran position was declared in the Confession of

Augsburg, and the year before he had provided his followers with the Short Catechism which summarized their faith and daily practice. In 1520 Luther had appealed to the German Nobility, and some of the princes, looking for an excuse to break the Holy Roman Empire, took up his cause. There began a series of wars of religion which were to drag on and affect every country in Europe for the next century and a half. The first attempt to create an alliance of Protestant forces failed when, at Marburg in 1529, Luther found himself unable to agree with Zwingli, the Swiss reformer, on the doctrine of the Eucharist. But, despite heavy odds against them, some of the German princes managed to establish their independence, and, though there was some changing of sides in the ensuing struggle, in several principalities there emerged a reformed Church. In Lutheran areas there was variety of church organization, but allegiance to the Pope was broken, medieval superstitions were swept away and the reformers took their stand on the Bible and the doctrine of Justification by Faith. Above all, Luther had given back to ordinary men and women real, personal religion. It was for this, and not just for the sake of a theological wrangle, that he had risked his life, defying the united authority of Pope and Emperor. It was for this, and not for any political cause—he was not a revolutionary and the Peasants' Revolt of 1524 shocked him—that he appealed to his countrymen for support. It was for this that he threw an inkpot at the devil. It was for this that he poured out an endless stream of writing: the translation of the Bible, his hymns, the Catechisms, his Table Talk, commentaries and pamphlets. It was for this that he preached, and, when his opponents attacked the Protestants with charges of immorality and lawlessness, for this that he urged his followers to show by the quality of their lives the proof of their faith.

The second stage of the Reformation was reached in Switzerland. To Zwingli belongs the honour of being the pioneer, but his attempt at reform did not go as deep as others, and it was Calvin who, in the second generation, really gave solidity to the new cause. A man of outstanding intellect and personality, for many years he directed the Reformation in France as well as in Geneva, and his letters and various writings are remarkable for their pastoral care as well as for their theological brilliance. He was the first, in his *Institutes*, to provide Protestantism with a fully worked out system of thought capable of standing comparison with the traditions of Rome. He set up in Geneva a new system of church government, providing a thoroughly practicable alternative to episcopacy, and the Presbyterian system was to become one of the great formative influences of modern history. Geneva itself became a sanctuary for Protestants persecuted in other countries and the most influential school of Protestant thought in Europe. Calvin's régime was based on rigid Augustinian theology grounded in belief in the sovereignty of God, and, in practice, it was often as harsh as its rival. But great strength and resolution were needed if the power of Rome was to be challenged, and, for the bitterness of the struggle that followed, all parties must bear equal blame. Calvin has been the centre of so much controversy through the years that we sometimes forget the man behind his teaching. The Venetian ambassador said of him in 1561: 'He is a man of extraordinary authority, who by his mode of life, his doctrine and his writings, rises superior to all the rest.' And it is the judgement of a later historian of France that Calvin influenced that country simply because he was the most Christian man of his generation.

The third stage of the struggle may be represented by the course of events in England. Here, through the expediency of Henry VIII's matrimonial and foreign policy, the increasing Protestantism of Edward and the reversion to Catholicism of Mary, the compromise of Elizabeth and the Civil War under the Stuarts, there emerged a third type of church. This was essentially a national institution, separated from Rome but preserving our episcopacy and a largely Catholic form of worship—the Book of Common Prayer is really the heart of the Anglican Church—and yet, to a large extent Protestant in theology. Though closely linked with crown and parliament, this church was to prove itself capable of great adaptability, as future events in America and the British Empire proved. It claims to have done away with medieval superstition and to rely largely upon Scripture and the tradition of the early Fathers, and it has always sought to establish friendly relations with other churches with similar claims, especially the Eastern Orthodox Church. But it was a compromise born of long struggle, and in many ways that has been its strength. A typical Anglican parson, the poet George Herbert, claimed that its justification was that it was 'Neither too mean, nor yet too gay' and that it had no 'Outlandish looks'.

But there is more to the history of the religious struggle in England than that. A fourth type of churchmanship was to arise which was to be of considerable influence in the future. Those who could not see their way to acceptance of royal dictation in matters of faith, became known as Separatists or Independents. Taking their stand on the New Testament these men advanced the theory of the 'gathered church', and believed that the congregation of worshippers in any place was entirely self-sufficient under the guidance of the Spirit of God. They insisted that Christ alone was Head of the Church, and, against all other claims of authority, they set themselves to defend 'the Crown Rights of the Redeemer'. Moreover, they held that the reformation of religion in England was not going fast or far enough and so they set about 'reformation without tarrying for anie'. Some of these, forced by persecution into exile in Holland and other places in Europe, came into contact with another independent group, the Anabaptists. These pioneers had been oppressed by Catholic and Protestant authorities alike for their opposition to State control of any kind and for their extreme statement of the Protestant position. It is clear, too, that in some of their communities moral and other extravagances had arisen. But the main effect of their meeting with the English Independents was to raise the question of Believer's Baptism in which they deeply believed. From this point the English Independents split into two, the Baptists accepting the Anabaptist view, and the Congregationalists adhering to infant baptism. In 1620 some of the

Independents, the Pilgrim Fathers, set sail for America, hoping there to be able to set up their ideal of church and society, free of persecution, but many others stayed to continue the struggle in England. All were united in following the belief of one of their leaders, John Robinson: 'I am verily persuaded, the Lord hath more Truth yet to break forth out of His holy Word'. The number of independent sects increased during the Civil War, and for most of the time the Independents found themselves fighting alongside the Scots and English Presbyterians against the king and bishops. The triumph of Cromwell and the New Model Army actually put the Independents in the ascendancy for a few years, but the alliance of Independents and Presbyterians was an uneasy one, and, though Cromwell privately believed in toleration, the only way to keep order in the country was by a dictatorship. This brought a reaction against the army and the Independents, and it now appeared that the decisive question was the position of the Presbyterians. On Cromwell's death they decided to support the return of the Stuarts and hoped for a further modification of the Anglican Church which would enable episcopacy and presbyterianism to co-exist to the exclusion of Independency. After the Restoration of 1660 and the return of episcopacy the now triumphant Anglicans would not, however, hear of 'comprehension', and, by the Act of Uniformity of 1662, the Presbyterians found themselves in their turn ejected from the Church of England. Their abandonment of the Independents had thus not had the hoped-for result. The Presbyterians, instead of coming to terms with the Anglicans, found that they had to side with their first allies, and it was this final rejection by the Established Church of both Presbyterians and Independents which was decisive. So many people were now outside the national Church that these Non-conformists, as they were called, became an important and influential section of the British people. For a time the attempt was made to suppress them by the Clarendon Code, but eventually their existence had to be recognized, and the Toleration Act of 1689 gave them liberty of worship, although it was not until the nineteenth century that they recovered all their civil rights. This set the pattern for the future development of the religious, and incidentally much of the social and political, tradition in England.

The importance of this development was not confined to England, but greatly influenced America as well. Here an entirely new religious situation was coming into being. The first missionaries to America had been Catholic, but they had by no means established their influence all over the continent, and there was plenty of room for others. The seventeenth century saw, in fact, a great migration of people from nearly all the countries of Europe to America. Many of them were refugees fleeing from the apparently endless religious persecutions on both sides at home, but later commercial interests entered into the race as well, so that in the end an extraordinary series of colonies was established all along the east coast of North America, in which all sorts and conditions of people lived side by side and every type of churchmanship was represented. There followed the wars by which the colonists won their independence and then, about the middle of the eighteenth century, the great move West which was really to lay the foundations of the American nation. This was accompanied by what is known as the Great Awakening when the Christian colonists, who hitherto had been only concerned with the fight for existence and independence, began to realize their missionary responsibilities and to preach the gospel, not only to the Indians and to the slaves who were being imported from Africa, but also to those large numbers of their own kind who had come to America for other than religious reasons. In the mid-nineteenth century there was a Second Great Awakening, the number of Christians on the continent was greatly increased, and the task of making America a Christian country has continued into this century. Because of the position of America in world affairs today, this history of the Church in America is one of the most important facts in modern history, and the separation of Church and State in the American constitution is due, not only to the Independency of many of the early Protestant settlers, but also to the exceptional variety of religious groups which established themselves in the New World, so that no one group achieved a clear ascendency for its own particular view.

It will be clear from the foregoing history of Europe and America that questions of toleration did not at first enter very much into the religious struggle. In some cases, as in that of the Peace of Augsburg in 1555, which brought to a temporary end the fighting in Germany, the only solution found was that citizens must accept the religion of their ruler. In the case of France, toleration was at first granted to the Protestant Huguenots by the Edict of Nantes, but that edict was revoked in 1685 and the Huguenots for the most part fled the country. In Germany and elsewhere meanwhile further fighting had resulted in the Treaty of Westphalia of 1648 which more or less settled for the rest of our period the lines of demarcation between Catholic and Protestant countries. In England, as we have seen, the Act of Toleration of 1689 at last gave the right to Non-conformists to worship as they wished, but they were regarded as second-class citizens, and it was not until the nineteenth century that the last act disqualifying them from service of the crown and education at the universities was removed from the statute book. Both Catholics and Protestants tended to retire into their own shells, and Protestants on the Continent of Europe tended to develop a scholasticism of their own as arid as that of the Catholic Church in the later Middle Ages. The most fruitful developments in church life were taking place in other parts of the world than the ancient centre of Christendom, and this was due, not only to the history of America, but also to the work of many sects—Pietists, Moravians and Quakers, for instance—whose missionary zeal and Christian witness often put the established churches to shame. The courage of the sectarians was tremendous and began to win recognition, so that by the end of the seventeenth century an increasing number of writers were suggesting that toleration was the only solution. Conscientious scruples must be recognized, and in most Protestant countries, at least, this has come to be accepted. At the same time, especially in America, the resistance of Independents has set a pattern for Protestantism which has led to the proliferation of sects, and there were occasions upon which people divided on minor issues with a corresponding weakening of the strength of Protestant witness and to the confusion of those who seek the truth. This has been the unhappy result of the grudging tolerance that was eventually granted often only because men were tired of fighting.

The religious awakening of America in the eighteenth century has been mentioned, but this was only one part of a surge of evangelism which affected the life of a great number of churches and countries. Of particular importance, since it has become, along with the Baptist Church, one of the two largest Protestant denominations in the world, is the rise of Methodism. Beginning as a society within the Church of England, in about two hundred years it has swept round the world, and, in the process, it has adopted a variety of forms. In Britain it has been broadly presbyterian, though in some branches lay men and women have played an unusually important part, while in America there have been episcopal varieties for the most part. The Methodist witness has been fundamentally Protestant, but it has added to this a renewed concern for something very like the old Catholic idea of the life of holiness, though Wesley had explored and rejected the old way of the mystics and made a fresh approach to the subject, basing it firmly on biblical doctrine and evangelical experience. John Wesley also gave to his people a very close organization, and even those who broke away to form branches of the original movement adhered closely to the original scheme, giving laymen a large part in the societies as local preachers, stewards, class leaders and so on. There has always been considerable emphasis on the social message of the Church, and in some of its witness Methodism has been reminiscent of some of the earlier Puritan attitudes to life. Wesley emerges as a religious genius, in fact, because of his combination of evangelical zeal with extraordinary practical ability. He is in the true evangelical succession of Paul, Augustine, Luther and Calvin, and he had an advantage which none of the others had—a brother who co-operated with him. Charles Wesley saw to it that 'Methodism was born in song', and the songs have spread around the world. Like Luther, Wesley believed in a revival of real religion, and in an age of increasing scientific experiment he taught his people to give evidence of a faith that worked. Recently there has been a tendency for the various branches of Methodism to reunite, but the impetus of the Methodist movement also produced other forms of church life such as the Salvation Army, whose founder was originally a Methodist and also showed a great interest in the social service of the Church.

In some of its features Methodism has not been unique, but rather typical of a good deal of modern Protestantism. The increasing part played by the laity has led to the very important conception of the whole Church taking the whole gospel to the whole world. The contribution of Protestants to education and other social service has been considerable. In the Church of England this took the form of Christian Socialism, in the Free Churches it led to the rise in the nineteenth century of the nonconformist conscience which had a very practical effect in politics and society as well as leading to a type of puritanical piety so often and so unfairly criticized. But this development has been more noticeable in the English and American forms of Protestantism than in those which sprang from Europe, which explains to some degree the atheistic nature of much of the liberalism and socialism of the Continent. The socialist parties on the Continent could never claim, for instance, as a Labour leader in Britain recently claimed, that the labour and trade union movements were in origin more Methodist than Marxist.

Another feature of Protestant church life which might also be mentioned is the growth of the place of the congregational hymn in church services. Luther, Watts, Wesley, Sankey and Moody, are only a few of the names which may be mentioned to illustrate how Protestants have set their faith to music and encouraged their members to use this method of learning and propagating their religion. And this development grew, of course, from the Protestant emphasis on the Bible as the ultimate source of religious authority. The great majority of hymns are the expression in verse of the great experimental truths of the Christian religion and its Book of books. As one authority has stated, it is since the Reformation that the Bible has become the Book of books for Englishmen—and, one must now add, for Americans and others as well. It is not surprising, therefore, that Protestants have also taken a great interest in the formation of Bible societies for the propagation of the faith. We shall return to this subject, but ought to mention now the work of such pioneers as Dr Thomas Bray and his co-founders of the Society for the Propagation of Christian Knowledge in 1698 and the Society for the Propagation of the Gospel in 1701.

At a different level there have been evidences of a growing concern with churchmanship among the Churches arising from the Reformation. In movements that might easily have degenerated into mere sectarianism, there have been those who have been anxious to insist that the Protestant has his place in the true Catholic Church. Some of the discussions of this matter have been provoked, in England at any rate, by the repercussions of the Oxford Movement in the Established Church in the nineteenth century. This movement was a High Church reaction against the excessive individualism of the time, and it is unfortunate that it tended to be critical of Evangelicals, for that only led to the counter-charge that it was itself too Catholic. But the contribution of Newman and its other leaders, the bringing of the subject into the centre of Christian discussion, and other tendencies such as the modern liturgical movement among the churches of Europe, show how one of the features of modern Reformation churches is a new concern with worship and the sacramental element of Christian life. These developments have caused much excitement in church circles, and, as a result, the final observation may be made that among Protestants the lines of churchmanship do not run, as in the earlier days, between the denominations so much as across the old denominational boundaries.

THE COUNTER-REFORMATION AND THE DEVELOPMENT OF ROMAN CATHOLICISM

Although Protestantism is now established as a separate and distinct part of the World Church, it did not appear at first that this must necessarily be the result of Luther's protest. Many on the Catholic side acknowledged that there was some force in some of his criticism, and, since the idea of the unity of the Church was so firmly held in Rome, the hope was that the Lutherans might be kept within the Church as the Franciscans had been, rather than be ejected as heretics. Indeed, until the Council of Ratisbon in 1541, the possibility of a settlement always seemed possible. But Luther made it clear that he did not feel that his points had been met, and his refusal to compromise allowed the reactionaries in the Roman Church, by this time growing in strength, to insist that the rebels must be dealt with.

One weapon employed was that of the Inquisition, already, as we have seen, used against earlier heretics, especially in Spain. It was now put under the direction of cardinals, and was at first used mainly in Italy itself. There had been disturbing signs of sympathy with Luther not far from Rome, but so thoroughly was this method employed that by 1572 the reforming party in Italy had been completely overcome. The Inquisition continued to be used throughout Catholic countries during the religious wars, and it is difficult to understand how Christians could employ such methods of torture and death against their fellows, though it must always be remembered, as we have seen in the case of Cavlinism, that all the faults were not on one side. The bitterness of the religious struggle aroused cruelty and harshness all round.

The second weapon created by the Roman Church was a number of new orders based, though with a new emphasis on obedience to the Pope, on vows similar to those which had been found so effective with the monks and friars. These were

F

the Theatines, Capuchins, Jesuits and the like. The Jesuits became the outstanding order of this type, and were originally a group of young men who had committed themselves to missionary work. But while Loyola and his friends waited for a ship to carry them East, it was suggested to them that they should become agents of the Inquisition, and, from this beginning, there came into being the order which above all placed itself under an almost military discipline in the hands of the Pope. Their subsequent history has, in fact, been chequered, as we shall see. Even within the Catholic Church there were those who felt uneasy about the casuistical methods employed, and the fact that in obedience to orders they were prepared to argue that the end always justified the means caused considerable criticism. In the meantime, however, men such as these who were ready to place themselves unreservedly under papal orders were ideal instruments for the purpose of furthering papal policy. Some of them indulged in underground politics and plotted against Protestant rulers, as Parsons did against Elizabeth I of England. Others were more saintly, gave themselves to the more spiritual work of saving souls, and, like Edmund Campion in 1581, paid for it with their lives. When one considers the bravery and persever-ance with which they applied themselves to their calling, and when one remembers the number of them who became martyrs in Protestant countries and on the mission field, one can only regret that many of them allowed themselves to pursue such dubious policies.

The third weapon for the fight against Protestantism was the Council of Trent, which met in a series of sessions from 1545 to 1563. These sessions provided an opportunity for a thorough examination of the whole of Catholic faith and practice, but, although certain reforms were achieved, the total effect of the Council was entirely reactionary. The Protestant doctrines of Sin, Grace and the Bible were condemned. The practice of granting Indulgences, which had been the match to start the whole blaze and which was, in fact, questioned by some Catholics, was defended without any concession. The Papacy once again emerged from a great council absolutely triumphant, and there was no question of placing any conciliar limitation upon papal supremacy. A Profession of Faith for converts was drawn up which, with very few additions, remains the formula still in use by Catholics to this day. The Council was a complete vindication of the Catholic position at its most unbending.

With these weapons in hand, the papacy launched on a campaign to recover the ground it had lost. It was almost entirely successful. Nearly all the territories in Germany, Austria and Poland which had gone over to the Protestants were regained, the development of Calvinism in France was arrested, and, as we have seen, was in the end to be cut off altogether until modern times. This was to be the beginning of a revival of Catholicism in France and the dawn of the golden age of the Church in Spain. The only areas which really escaped the Counter-Reformation were the Protestant cantons of Switzerland, Scandinavia, Holland and Great Britain. The Dutch only escaped by the skin of their teeth and the genius of the House of Orange, and, if Mary had had her way or the Armada had succeeded, England might also have had to submit. So small was the margin by which Protestantism survived.

The policy of aggression was backed, moreover, by a genuine attempt to reform the clergy. One of the chief complaints of the critics had been the low standard of competence and morals of the clergy. These complaints were dealt with, through education and discipline, with almost complete success, and the new orders helped greatly by the new standard of devotion which they set. The orders also embarked on triumphant missionary activity, so that, not only did it appear that the old world was returning to its former allegiance, but also it seemed that the New World was going to be captured for Catholicism. The Roman Church has never been so strong as she was in the year 1700.

Yet the Catholic world was not completely united. In the years that followed disputes were to arise which considerably weakened the effectiveness of the Counter-Reformation. Two attempts to revive Augustinianism in the Church, one by Baius in Belgium and the other by Jansen and Pascal in France, were resisted by the Semi-Pelagians led by the Jesuits, and in each case the Jesuits triumphed. In later years there was something of a reaction, too, against the centralizing policy of the papacy. This was particularly strong in France, where the Gallican party stood out for a certain amount of independence against the Ultramontanes. In other words, the centralizing party fell foul of certain national and political feelings once more, and when Napoleon dominated Europe the Pope had to come to special terms with him in the Concordat of 1801. This to some extent cleared up the difficulties raised by the French Revolution, and, during the nineteenth century, the Pope recovered a good deal of his former position. But similar questions continued to arise so that this matter of nationalism continues to be a subject demanding the frequent attention of the papacy. The other disputes were those which arose between the orders, and particularly those occasioned by the Jesuits. The other orders became jealous of their special relations with the centralizing party, contested the theories of probabilism and aequiprobabilism with which they sought to justify the means they adopted in their work, and cast grave suspicion on some of their missionary methods. The result of these feuds, reinforced by political difficulties in which the Jesuits sometimes found themselves, was that the order was suppressed in 1773. The chief effect of this was seriously to weaken the missionary work of the Roman Church at a time when Protestants were just beginning to become really active. But the order was restored in 1814, and since then has resumed and even increased its power and influence.

One sign of this was the increasing influence of the teaching of Liguori, a Jesuit theologian, who has really supplanted Augustine as the decisive voice in modern Catholic theology. It was under the influence of his teaching that the papalist party persuaded the Church to accept the dogma of the Immaculate Conception in 1854 and the dogma of Papal Infallibility in 1870. In the later years of the nineteenth century, therefore, there was no relaxing of the rigidity of the Roman Church, and confirmatory evidence of this was the declaration of condemnation of Anglican Ordinations by Pope Leo XIII. The only sort of unity which the Roman Church seemed willing to contemplate was that which involved going for a ride on the tiger.

Following the Council which declared for Papal Infallibility in 1870, there was a breakaway from Rome by a minority of Catholics who could not bring themselves to accept the new dogma. This group was led by Dollinger, a learned and respected leader of the church in Germany. 'As a Christian, as a theologian, as a historian, as a citizen,' he said, 'I cannot receive this doctrine.' The Old Catholics, as these and certain other similar groups are called, have never been a very large or popular community, perhaps because it is only too easy to represent them as ultra-conservative. Certainly Dollinger was not the reincarnation of Luther. But it is well to note the occasional signs of criticism of the absolutism of the papacy which have appeared from time to time in the history of Romanism.

It cannot be pretended that secessions have much disturbed the calm of the Roman Church. In more recent years, she has had to face also considerable political attacks, especially in countries turning to socialism or communism. It would appear, indeed, that opposition has served in many cases as a stimulus to renewed vigour. In western Europe, America, Africa, Australia and some parts of Asia, the Roman Church continues its advance, often more rapidly than other branches of the Church. And, of course, the Roman Church continues to be the largest single section of the Church Universal. It is this fact, as well as its long history, which leads the Roman to lean so heavily on the tradition of the Church and to suspect those who prefer Scripture and Experience as superior authorities. Even so, it is interesting to note recent encouragement of Bible reading and family prayers in certain areas of the Roman Church, and this is a side of the life of that church which must be set against her continuing and unfortunate intransigence in other areas. In recent months, too, there have been signs that Rome may be considering fresh possibilities in the realm of inter-Church relationships. The first reaction of successive popes to the formation of the World Council of Churches was entirely hostile, and Roman Catholics were forbidden to participate in any discussions on unity. But recently the new pope has announced the calling of an ecumenical council of his Church and has appointed an official to deal with matters of Christian unity. It is possible that observers, though not participants, may be exchanged between one council and the other. And Pope John has welcomed a friendly visit from the Archbishop of Canterbury. Such moves suggest that in the future Christians of all kinds may find ways for much greater co-operation than has been thought possible hitherto, but we must return to this matter of Church relationships later.

THE EASTERN ORTHODOX CHURCH

Christians brought up in the traditions of the West, whether they have remained within the Church of Rome or whether they have been Protestants against Rome, have always tended to have their thought dominated by the teaching and pattern of Church life which owes so much to the achievements of the western Church in the Dark and Middle Ages. It has been only too easy to forget that this is not the only form of Christianity, and to suggest that other forms are side channels of the main stream. But to think thus is to ignore the claim of the Eastern Orthodox Church that, in fact, it is she who maintains the earliest traditions of church life, and that she has done so in an unbroken succession. After all there were Christians in the East before there were Christians in Rome, and, even if it be admitted that Constantinople assumed a position of leadership later in the day than the other great original centres of authority in the early Church and that she cannot claim apostolic foundation, nevertheless the accidents of history did eventually result in the leadership of the East being accorded to Constantinople with the consequence that she gathered to herself all the earliest traditions of Christianity. These traditions she has preserved through all the vicissitudes of history, and, so the argument runs, it is therefore in Eastern Orthodoxy rather than in the western variations that the true pattern of the Church is to be found. This may not be the last word in the argument, but at least it is sufficient reminder that there is a very large body of Christians in the world which continues to the present day and has a history rather different from that which we have so far considered.

The threat of the Turkish Empire to Europe, and with it the threat of Islam to Christianity, came to an end soon after the fall of Constantinople in 1453. In the modern period pressure gradually relaxed, and the Eastern Orthodox Church began to recover in lands which the Turks had been dominating. As we have noted previously, despite the Schism of East from West, communication between the two had never ceased entirely, even if it was largely because of the activity of Roman missionaries who were trying to secure the allegiance of eastern churches to the supremacy of Rome. So, in the Reformation period, Christians in the East remained aware of what was going on in the West, and at one time considerable interest was aroused in the points that the Protestants were raising. That this was more than seeing the possibility of finding new allies against the ancient Roman rival seems to be indicated by the fact that in the seventeenth century the Patriarch Cyril Lucar was strongly attracted to Calvinism and proposed reforms in the Orthodox Church which would have involved acceptance of some of the teaching of the reformers. The only result of this, however, was that a combination of patriotism and Jesuit activity in the East secured a defeat of Lucar's policy, and the Council of Jerusalem in 1672 not only rejected Calvinism but also went to the other extreme by accepting the Roman doctrine of transubstantiation. This was a tremendous victory for the Jesuits, and represented, in fact, the high-water mark of Roman influence in the East. On the whole, however, the very success of the Jesuits proved their undoing, for most people in the East resented Roman interference and a reaction set in. The Jesuits began to meet with increasing resistance and it was not long before once again Orthodoxy became identified with patriotism.

Meanwhile, the missionary work of the Church had been so successful that a strong part of Orthodoxy had been established in Russia. In 1589, owing to political pressure to a large degree, the Russian Orthodox Church separated itself from Constantinople, and this is the sign of the way in which Constantinople as well as Rome was being affected by the new nationalism. In this case, the alliance between Church and State did not work out to the advantage of the Church, and, as in Constantinople itself Caesaropapalism had always threatened to weaken the effectiveness of the Church, so in Russia the Church increasingly tended to become merely a department of State. Why this tendency should have been so marked in Eastern Orthodoxy and the Church less successful than in other areas in maintaining its independence, is not clear. No doubt it was partly due to a different political and social situation, but partly also it seems to have been because of the early history of the Church in Constantinople. Here, in the early days, Constantine and his successors had been called in to arbitrate in the bitter theological controversy which had threatened to divide the Church, and this appeal to the emperors, combined with their own natural inclination to be in absolute control of the affairs of their realms, seems to have been sufficient to stamp a pattern of domination upon the Church such as never developed to the same degree in Rome and the West.

It is wrong to think, however, that there were no protests against this situation. The most notable was that of the Patriarch Nikon, who tried to assert the independence of the Church at the same time as he proposed reform of her liturgy. The liturgical reform was successful, but the attempt to establish independence was not, and in fact the Emperor Peter the Great eventually decided in 1721 to abolish the office of Patriarch and to rule the church by a Holy Synod, which, of course, the imperial family took good care to control. This was the situation in Russia right up to the Revolution, and the militant atheism of the revolutionaries would no doubt have been greatly modified if Nikon had had his way. He had used arguments similar to those of medieval popes—that the Church was the sun and the State only the moon—in his attempt to deny to the emperors the right of dictation in Church affairs, but his fight for independence was occasioned by his desire to give the Church the authority to put her own house in order. If he had been allowed to discipline the clergy and to raise the standard of their education, as he planned, Rasputin and the Russian clergy would not have fallen victim to the bitterness and hatred of later years. It was a tragedy, too, that Nikon was not wholeheartedly supported by the clergy, and that the attempts at reform resulted in a split in the Church. It was largely on the grounds of the liturgical innovations that, in the seventeenth century, those who called themselves the Old Believers became an independent minority. In 1914 they represented about four million of the Russian population, and in the meantime the running fight that had been going on with the established Church—in which the government had often had to intervene—only served to weaken the unity, strength and authority of the Church.

As in other parts of the eastern world, so in Russia the agents of Rome appeared. From the time of Peter the Great when the policy of Russia was westward-looking and many avenues of communication were established with the favour and consent of the government, missionaries from the West were positively encouraged to enter Russia. The Jesuits as usual appeared on the scene, and, though without success, tried to repeat in Russia the policy which had been so successful elsewhere of establishing Uniate churches. The situation changed entirely with the Napoleonic Wars which revived all the old Slav suspicions of the West. Russia went back into her shell, and in 1819 the Jesuits found themselves banished from the country. As in so many other places, they had been over-zealous for Rome and had outstayed their welcome.

The later nineteenth century saw new developments in Russia which, however, came too late and were on too small a scale immediately to affect the situation. Nevertheless in 1867 a translation of the Bible in the vernacular appeared, and by the year 1870 a noticeable number of Baptists had established themselves. In addition to their more normal witness, these Protestants contributed largely to a movement against image worship in churches which was a fresh point of dispute at this time. The call for reform of various kinds was beginning to be heard with increasing frequency, and much of it gathered eventually around the famous figure of Tolstoy. But, despite his considerable influence, most of the leaders of the Church remained blind and deaf to what was going on around them, and the close identification of the established Church with the autocratic government was maintained.

So, when the Revolution came, the Church, or at least thousands of its leaders and priests, went down with the rulers with whom they were identified, and, although the removal of the old régime brought about the restoration of the Patriarchate, in 1917 the deliberate anti-Church policy of the Bolsheviks was put into full operation. This has not succeeded in destroying the Church, and the Communists have used a variety of methods to weaken the strength of the Christian forces that have survived. In 1922-3, for instance, a group of progressive priests, determined to maintain good relations with the government, broke away to form what is known as the Renovated Church. The government naturally encouraged this division of Christian forces, and in 1927 it was reckoned that about a third of the parishes in Russia had joined the movement. The full story of the Church in Russia in the twentieth century is hardly, of course, yet known, but despite opposition and persecution, Christian witness is still maintained in Baptist as well as Orthodox churches.

The Orthodox Church is represented, of course, in other countries, Yugo-slavia, Greece, Rumania and Bulgaria, for instance, and there are other communities, some of them exiles, scattered in other parts of the world. Their history in modern times has been similar to that of Constantinople, with the struggle for restoration after the decline of the Turkish Empire, the establishment of independent patriarchates, rivalry between various monastic orders, and involvement in world wars and their aftermath as features in the story. What is of great interest is that, in contrast with the Roman Church, representatives of these Churches have taken part in the world-wide discussions of Churches of all kinds on faith and unity, which have taken place in the twentieth century.

THE EXPANSION OF THE CHURCH

The growth of the Church in modern times has been one of the most remarkable phenomena in history. Christians of all types have taken part in the expansion, and the result is that Christianity, instead of being merely a Mediterranean religion, as it was until the sixteenth century, has become a world religion with representatives in nearly every country. No previous expansion of the Church can compare with the expansion of the last four and a half centuries, and no other religion has shown the capacity to appeal to people of so many different races and cultures. Christianity is, in fact, the world religion, and it seems as though only the challenge of the Church has provoked other ancient religions to attempt a similar policy of development in recent times. Whether other religions will show the same resilience as Christianity remains to be seen, but meanwhile it remains the fact that Christianity alone has shown so far the ability to appeal to the world. All sections of the Church have taken part in the expansion. The Eastern Orthodox Church made its contribution largely in the countries neighbouring its original centres and made slow but steady and considerable advance in the great European and Asian land mass. But the outstanding development took place westwards, and it is with this part of the story that we are chiefly concerned.

From 1500 to the middle of the eighteenth century, largely for political reasons, the missionary work of the Church was chiefly in the hands of the Roman Catholics. The chief single cause of this was that the leading sea powers of the day were Catholic—Spain, Portugal and France—and it was the discovery of the ocean trade routes which enabled expansion to take place. Instead of having to try to batter down the defences of Islam by the eastern land routes, Christian countries now discovered that what had appeared to be a back door only was the gateway to the world. The ancient enemy, Islam, could thus be circumnavigated and, whereas Islam had hitherto barred the way to further progress, lands which had been inaccessible were now wide open to the pioneer.

In the mood of confidence engendered by the success of the Counter-Reformation, the Catholics seized their opportunity, and the dangerous split which had taken place in the shrunken and weakened Christendom of the later Middle Ages, instead of being the catastrophe which some had feared, proved in the end to be a great stimulus to new effort. Catholics as well as Protestants had been brought to see the need for real religion, and it is to the credit of the Catholics that they immediately responded to the call of the New World and sought to carry the Christian religion to its peoples. Though, of course, the movement of the Church ran parallel to a great extent with the imperialist ambitions of the great powers of the day and it is only too easy to sneer at the Church's participation in political and economic aggrandizement, it is important to realize that there was genuine religious concern as well. When imperialistic enterprises were abandoned or their appetite sated, missionaries often remained to carry on the Church's work and normally penetrated much farther than the adventurers. The Christian monarchs of Spain, in particular, took very seriously the religious implications of their policies and spent a great amount of their resources in support of missionary work. The popes were constant in their encouragement of evangelism, as they had been at their best from the time of Gregory I. Above all, the Catholic Church had at its disposal in the new orders founded at the time of the Counter-Reformation a source of devoted man power exactly suited to the needs of the day.

So vast was the scale of operations that it is impossible to follow it in any detail, but by 1750 the Catholics had built up large Christian communities in North and South America, and these were added to by smaller achievements in Africa, India and the East Indies. The missions, of course, had varying fortunes, and were not established without much cost, in life as well as in resources. The whole tale is one of great courage and the life of Francis Xavier, a Jesuit who travelled from one country to another, always farther east until he died on the doorstep of China, is typical of the spirit which inspired the men of this age. If there was a weakness in these missions it lay in the identification of the missionaries with their imperialistic and commercial fellow travellers. Nevertheless, the coming of the Church did help to soften to some extent the impact of western civilization on its bewildered victims. By such measures as the Laws of the Indies, the missionaries sought to remind their fellow countrymen of their obligations to their fellow men, and, on the whole, the Church had an honourable record in protecting those who might have been exploited even more ruthlessly than they were. But the Catholics on the whole did not give sufficient attention to the creation of indigenous churches in their newly won territories. The missionary movement remained for too long a campaign directed from hundreds of miles away, and the Church was slow in admitting nationals to the priesthood. The seriousness of this mistake was exposed when the Jesuit order was suppressed. Though the suppression brought to an end the wrangles which had developed between the orders about the methods used by the Jesuits, their withdrawal disastrously weakened the resources available for the work, and in some areas there was a relapse into paganism because of a lack of leadership.

Before 1750 hardly any missionary work stands to the credit of the Protestant churches. The seventeenth century had seen the setting up of Protestant colonies along with others in North America, but their purpose was not missionary. The first Protestants to arrive in the New World were refugees, they were seeking safety, not adventure, and their outlook was still that of their friends at home. Here, for most of this period, Protestants were still fighting for their lives. All available resources were poured into the struggle for existence and recognition; the Protestant countries were not yet great sea powers; the organization of their churches had nothing to offer comparable with the Catholic orders; and some of their theology was not of a type to inspire missionary effort. In the middle of the eighteenth century, however, a great change took place. The Dutch and the British supplanted Spain and France as the great sea powers, so that the advantage here now lay with the Protestants. The wars of religion were over and Protestant countries now recognized in Europe could devote their energies to other spheres. There followed the period of the Great Awakening in America and of the Evangelical Movement and the birth of Methodism in Britain. The Protestants now entered, therefore, into the general missionary movement of the Church, and they took it up with such enthusiasm that in the nineteenth century they were to outstrip the efforts of the Catholics.

Much of the inspiration for missionary work at this time came originally from the Moravians—John Wesley himself was greatly indebted to them. They were a Protestant community with roots in the pre-Reformation work of John Hus, but had been driven out of Bohemia and Moravia in the seventeenth century. They found refuge at Herrnhut in Saxony and, under the leadership of Count Zinzendorf, became a sort of Protestant monastic order. Every member of the community was a potential missionary, and it was not long before their work began to spread all over the world. The most significant development was the establishment of a settlement in America, which, on Christmas Day 1741, was named Bethlehem. But it was not the Moravians only who set to work; soon all denominations were deeply involved. In some cases the seizure of territories which had been in the hands of Catholics meant that these lands and their churches turned to Protestantism, in others, though Protestant churches were, of course, established, the Catholics were not driven out and the development of both Churches continued side by side. But Protestants were not content simply with taking over lands already won, the end of the century saw the foundation of large numbers of missionary societies in Europe, England and America, and missionaries began to pioneer in areas which had hitherto been untouched. A feature of the Protestant missionary enterprise was that, whereas Catholic missions had received a good deal of support from kings and governments, the new effort was supported almost entirely by voluntary subscription. In some ways this makes the subsequent achievements all the more remarkable, but it proved that more than ever before the whole Church was committed to the task of carrying the Christian religion to the four corners of the earth.

With this inspiration the nineteenth century became the Great Century as far as the expansion of the Christian Faith is concerned. The conversion of the peoples of North America was, as we have seen, carried on at an increasing rate and the successes achieved here constituted the greatest single advance numerically. David Livingstone and other missionaries were the first men to open up the Dark Continent of Africa. The bridge-heads already established in Asia were expanded, and many new countries in the continent, especially China and Japan, for the first time developed Christian communities of significant size. In the islands of the Pacific and the southern seas and in Australasia new colonies of the Faith were established. It was in this period that Christianity really became recognized as a world religion. The preaching of the gospel always brought with it hospitals, schools and other agencies for the advance-ment of primitive peoples, and the work of the Bible societies was of immense importance. In fact, the work of translating the Scriptures into the vernacular of all the peoples now demanding it has been the greatest single contribution made by any body of any sort to the literacy and education of the world.

The Protestants, because of their individualistic beliefs, were not so slow as the Catholics had been to encourage members of the younger churches to undertake roles of leadership. Although the development was uneven, yet in the nineteenth century and even more so in the twentieth, for this and other reasons, there has been much more emphasis on making the new churches indigenous to the countries in which they were growing. In some areas, such as South India, mass movements to Christianity took place, and, although in some areas, because of the poverty of the people, problems of leadership remained, the foundations were so well laid in the nineteenth century that in the twentieth the pace of the transformation of missions into churches in their own right has rapidly increased.

This has underlined the fact that the Church is deeply involved in the emerging national consciousness of many parts of the world, especially Africa and Asia. It has to be admitted that the areas of greatest success of the Church's missionary work were those in which the missionary was dealing with primitive forms of animism, and that when he was faced with a well-established religion, Mohammedanism, Hinduism or Buddhism, progress was much slower and even in some cases almost absent. It is in these areas, moreover, that the very success of Christianity has stimulated a counter-offensive on the part of other faiths, and when this is allied to modern nationalism, the Christian convert of today finds himself charged, as previous generations have been, with a lack of patriotism on the score of religion. So in new situations new Christians are seeking to prove once again that their faith is not a betrayal but the true hope of new life.

No account, however brief, of the expansion of the Church in modern times would be complete without reference to the extraordinary heroism of the missionaries and their converts. Caricatures of the pioneers as bible-punching imperialists give no real picture of the devotion and self-sacrifice of thousands of men and women. Some of them, like Thomas Coke, dying on board ship on his way to the East, never reached their destination. Some of them fell speedy victims to the climate and the diseases of the countries to which they went. In thirty years, for instance, at the beginning of the nineteenth century, a hundred and ten missionaries died at their posts in 'the white man's grave' in West Africa, and many more had been invalided home. Some of them were murdered, like John Williams the great pioneer in the islands of the Pacific who met his death on Erromanga in the New Hebrides in November 1839. And many more, who gave a lifetime of service to new lands, never saw their native land again once they had left its shores. These pioneers were all inspired by the same spirit as led William Carey to say: 'Attempt great things for God, expect great things from God.' Nor was it the missionaries alone who suffered. New converts found themselves threatened and persecuted, and many gave their lives for their new faith. Wesleydale, New Zealand, was, for instance, destroyed in Maori raids, and other newly formed Christian communities suffered in the same way all round the world. In recent years there have been Kikuyu martyrs in Mau Mau territory, and no one knows how many martyrs there have been in countries like Russia and China. Even where there has not been the threat of death, society has cut the Christians out of its midst. In some parts it has been the custom to hold a funeral service when a member of a family has become a Christian, and the convert has known that, at very least, he is cut off from home and family for ever. All this is part of an heroic tale, and it is well to remember that the last four centuries have seen courage and self-sacrifice as great as those of any period in the Church's history. And the end is not yet. The blood of the martyrs is still the seed of the Church.

Whatever the difficulties, the facts remain. As a result of the missionary activity of the last century and a half in particular, Christianity is now the most widely extended religion of the world. Despite the apparent decline of the influence of the Church in some of her ancient strongholds, there are more Christians in the world than there have ever been. The world wars have perhaps slowed down the rate of increase in the last few years, and the increase in the world's birth rate has certainly overtaken it, but Christianity has still attained a position of extraordinary potential and influence. In the process of expansion the Church has not only enormously increased in size, she has also changed to some extent in character. There are now as many non-Catholics as Catholics—for every three Roman Catholics, two Protestants and one Orthodox. And, above all, she has become less identified with one particular form of civilization. She is less western. She belongs now to the world.

THE ECUMENICAL MOVEMENT

The changed nature of the Church is particularly evident in a growing spirit of co-operation which has developed in recent years among Christians. It has been largely a movement among Protestants who, in earlier periods, tended to be separatist. But, although Roman Catholics have until very recently remained aloof, others, Orthodox and Coptic (Nestorian), have joined in as well. It has brought together denominations previously at loggerheads. It embraces older and younger churches, East and West. And the stimulus has been very largely the missionary activity of the universal Church just described. Critics of the Church have always been quick to point to the inconsistency of a profession of faith in one Lord with the actual facts of denominational history, but Christians have been equally concerned, and the twentieth century in particular seems at last to have provided the opportunity for a constructive instead of the negative approach of former centuries to this most intricate problem.

Co-operation can take many forms, and some of them began to appear in the nineteenth century and even earlier. In 1795 the London Missionary Society, a voluntary association of members of different churches, was inaugurated. This has since become predominantly Congregationalist, but it was an early example of the co-operation which has persisted in missionary circles and has been continued in the voluntary consultations of various interdenominational missionary boards. Bible and Tract Societies were another fruitful source of co-operative enterprise, representatives of many churches joining in the common task of providing translations of scriptures and other religious literature for the rapidly expanding Church. Work in Sunday-schools, and among students and youth in general, led to the creation of such bodies as the World Sunday School Association, the World's Committee of the Young Men's Christian Association, and the World Student Christian Federation. Many other similar examples could be given, but these will suffice to show the tendency towards co-operation, which so far, however, was of an entirely voluntary nature.

More significant has been the tendency in the twentieth century for various branches of the same denominational family, and, in one or two cases, even of churches of different denominations, to come together in organic unity. The United Church of Canada came into being in 1925 and was composed of Methodists, Congregationalists, and Presbyterians. The Church of Christ in China brought together the work of various missionary churches in 1927, and was followed by a similar Church in Japan in 1941. The Church of Scotland and the United Free Church of Scotland were joined in 1929. The various main branches of Methodism came together to form The Methodist Church, in Great Britain in 1932 and in the United States in 1939. The various Lutheran churches of America have similarly been brought together. The Church of South India, created in 1947, brought together former episcopal and non-episcopal churches, and has proved for this reason a great stimulus to the exploration of further possible unions of this kind. In fact, there is almost perpetual discussion going on at present within and between the various denominations to discover what further steps towards union may be arranged. All this is a sign of the realization of Christians that ancient denominational barriers which no longer have any real significance in the new situation of the Church in the modern world ought to be removed as speedily as possible.

This realization especially applied to the situation of the younger churches, so often the creation of a western denomination but no longer interested in the tales and battles of far off and long ago. The problem of these churches was to present Christianity, not denominationalism, to their people. So it was not surprising that from missionary circles came the lead which was to produce co-operation of quite new significance and importance.

In 1910, on the initiative of the World Student Christian Federation and many missionary societies, a Conference of 1,200 members assembled at Edinburgh. This conference was epoch-making. For the first time in the history of such consultations between the churches, the membership of the conference was not on a voluntary basis but consisted of officially delegated representatives of the participating bodies. It was more comprehensive than any previous conference. Anglo-Catholics joined with Evangelicals, and younger churches were represented along with the older. It met to concert missionary policy, though only in an advisory not a legislative capacity. As a result of the conference a Continuation Committee was established, and this led to the formation in 1921 of the International Missionary Council, which has continued to gather to itself through the years the support and participation of an increasing number of missionary bodies. A series of conferences has followed at Jerusalem in 1928, in Madras in 1938, in Ontario in 1947, in Germany in 1952 and in Ghana in 1958. The result has been a great deal of co-operative planning of the missionary work of a variety of churches and the sharing of many ecclesiastical and theological viewpoints. The younger churches themselves were given an increasing voice in the deliberations. By 1938, half the delegates, and since then more than half, were drawn from these churches, and this fact in itself is significant of the winds of change that are blowing in the Church.

Meanwhile, largely stimulated by the Edinburgh Conference and its consequences, new developments were set in train which were to lead to the foundation of the World Council of Churches. Two separate movements encouraged discussion between the churches. A World Conference on

Faith and Order was held at Lausanne in 1927 and was followed by a second meeting at Edinburgh in 1937 consisting of 414 official delegates from 122 different communions and 43 countries. The Universal Christian Council for Life and Work was also brought into being to stimulate thought and action on the application of Christian faith and principles to social and international problems, a tremendously important development of one side of the Church's life in modern times. It also held two conferences, one at Stockholm in 1925, and the other at Oxford in 1937. In many cases the participating churches appointed the same delegates to both of the 1937 meetings, so it was not surprising that in 1938 a body of representatives met at Utrecht to draft a constitution for what was to be known as the World Council of Churches. Whereas the International Missionary Council consisted of regional and national bodies, the World Council was to consist of representatives of churches, and was, therefore, ecclesiastical in structure and outlook. The Council would not have legislative powers, but it would provide an unprecedented opportunity for common study and action.

The coming of war prevented an immediate meeting, but a committee at Geneva maintained valuable communications between churches separated by conflict and undertook further work of preparation. As a result the first World Council of Churches met at Amsterdam in 1948. It consisted of representatives of over a hundred churches, and brought together not only almost all the major Protestant bodies of Europe, America and Australasia—Anglicans, Lutherans, Reformed, Presbyterians, Congregationalists, Baptists and Methodists—but also most of the younger churches of Africa and Asia. In addition there were representatives of the Eastern Orthodox and Old Catholic Churches as well as of the ancient Syrian Church of Malabar, the Nestorians, Swedenborgians, Salvation Army and Quakers. The bridging of the gap between Protestants and some of the Catholic churches was of great significance, and the only major absentee was the Church of Rome.

The Council has established contact with all manner of missionary and interdenominational bodies, and has gathered to itself an increasing amount of support from additional churches. By the time of its meeting at Evanston in 1954 its membership consisted of 163 different churches and ecclesiastical federations from nearly fifty countries, and included such newcomers as the Coptic Church. Roman Catholics still did not participate, and a great number of Eastern Orthodox churches have not yet found it possible for a variety of reasons, some of them political, to join in. Some Protestants, too, chiefly Lutherans, Anglo-Catholics and extreme conservatives among the Baptists and Presbyterians have held aloof. But despite this, the Council represents the greatest coming together of Christians of different shades of opinion that the world has ever known. The latest proposal is that the World Council of Churches and the International Missionary Council should join forces, and, when this is achieved, the forces working for unity will be further strengthened.

The result of all this discussion and activity has been such a considerable realignment of Christian forces as to bring very much to the forefront the new character of the Church which we have already noted. Parallel with inter-denominational developments has been running a growth of international grouping of the main denominations. Lambeth Conferences of the Anglican Church have been held since 1867. The World Alliance of Presbyterians came into being in 1875. Ecumenical Methodist Conferences have met frequently since 1881. The International Congregational Council was formed in 1891, and the Baptist World Alliance in 1905. These and other groupings have encouraged a discussion and sharing of ideas which all contribute to the general discussion of the life of the Universal Church, into which all churches seek to bring the best of their traditions. The new atmosphere has encouraged the anticipation of the Coming Great Church.

What shape the future history of the Church will take it is impossible to forecast, but the point is that it is not fixed but changing, and the problem for Christians is to discover how past traditions may be adapted to serve the present age. Conservative elements on both sides, Catholic and Protestant, look upon the development of the World Council of Churches with some misgiving and suspicion. In the Protestant section of the Church, in particular, it appears not unlikely that much discussion will have to be undertaken on such questions as those of the authority of the Bible and the nature of the Church, which, as we have already seen, have been the cause of many variations in Church life since the Reformation. Meanwhile, for the Roman Catholic and those of similar outlook, it has been difficult to envisage any development of the Church which is not in accord with the traditions of the past and especially with the exclusive claims to authority which has seemed essential to this type of churchmanship. Yet even in this section of the Church, though the signs are as yet only tentative, the new situation of the Church in the world does seem to have stimulated new questions, and, as we have seen, new suggestions and approaches have been made. Whether this will lead to any speedy steps towards co-operation and unity remains to be seen.

But, in the meantime, the discussion and experiment concerning co-operation and union go on at all levels and in all circles of the Church. In face of revolution, the challenge of materialism and the scientific outlook, Communism, modern nationalism and a possible counter-attack by other religions, Christians of all kinds are more conscious than ever before of belonging to one another. Not that the stimulus to Church unity has come from outside pressure only. Just as in the earliest centuries it was not persecution by the State which alone brought Christians together in self-defence, so, now as then, it is the growing life of the Church itself from within which leads Christians to seek to express their faith in universal and united terms as an essential witness to their belief in one Lord. The very success of the Church's advance in recent times, the spread of the Church into the entire world situation, has brought fresh problems and new responsibilities. The World Church, the great new fact of the twentieth century, as

Archbishop Temple called it, faces the world, and as the world changes the Church adapts herself to fresh needs. Successes may have been achieved, but for the Christian there remains an unfinished task. The question that lies behind all the modern developments and debates is still how the whole Church may take the whole gospel to the whole world. A modern cry is: 'Let the Church be the Church.'

Postscript

THE ATTEMPT has been made to tell the plain story of the Church with as little ecclesiastical or theological bias as possible. From this point of view the story is a historical account of ordinary as well as of outstanding people adopting a faith and seeking to share it with the rest of the world. The affairs of the world in which they lived and live are necessarily part of the story, and the development of the Church has often been more influenced than is sometimes recognized by contemporary events.

At the same time, the Christian Church has not only been moulded by the world, it has also to a considerable extent itself moulded the communities in which it has been set. Without the influence of Christianity, the history of mankind would have taken a very different course. To put it in other words the history of Christianity is really the story of the influence of Jesus of Nazareth in the lives of men. That influence is quite unique. A village carpenter from a comparatively small people has shaken the world more than the strongest dictator at the head of a great empire. He has, moreover, cast his spell on all sorts and conditions of men.

In our day, as in others, some have been eager to prove that the influence of Jesus is coming to an end. On the other hand, some Christians, seeking to read the signs of the times, declare with confidence that Jesus himself is about to come as Judge and end world history his way. Others of us, however, seeing how in our own day his Church has just become established as a fact of world history, believe that this is not the beginning of the end. It is, rather, the end of the beginning.

Books for Further Reading

A BRIEF LIST only is given, lest too long a list appear to threaten to kill with kindness. But some of the books suggested have their own bibliographies which, in their turn, may lead to further reading.

H. B. WORKMAN. *Persecution in the Early Church*

J. FOSTER. *Beginning from Jerusalem*
To All Nations

These two paperbacks give a vivid, popular account of the growth of the Church. Professor Foster has also produced a series of lectures offering an outline of Church History illustrated by film strips. This may be obtained from Common Ground (1951) Ltd., 44 Fulham Road, London, S.W.3.

J. W. C. WAND. *A History of the Early Church*

M. DEANESLY. *A History of the Medieval Church*

J. W. C. WAND. *A History of the Modern Church*

A useful series of reasonable length, though the third volume hardly does justice to the contribution of the Free Churches, especially in America.

K. S. LATOURETTE. *A History of Christianity*

About 1,500 pages, but a masterly survey of the whole story.

J. R. H. MOORMAN. *A History of the Church in England*

N. SYKES. *The English Religious Tradition*

E. A. PAYNE. *The Free Church Tradition in the Life of England*

For Methodism in particular, useful popular accounts are given in:

C. E. VULLIAMY. *John Wesley*

C. J. DAVEY. *The Methodist Story*

C. J. DAVEY. *The March of Methodism*

Index

(*This index is not exhaustive, but lists many of the people and places in this book.*)

Abelard, 56
Africa, 91, 93, 94, 95, 99
Aidan, 44
Alban, 16
Alcuin, 45
Alexander II, Pope, 54
Alexander VI, Pope, 64, 68
Alexandria, 34, 40
Alfred, King, 47, 54
Algiers, 50
Ambrose, 18
America, 72, 73, 74, 76, 91, 92, 93, 97, 99
Anabaptists, 72
Anselm, 55, 56
Anthony, 34
Antioch, 34, 40
Antoninus Pius, 15
Apollinarius, 27
Aquinas, 56
Arabia, 11
Arius, 26
Armenia, 11, 42, 60, 61
Asia, 93, 94, 99
Asia Minor, 11, 13, 16, 34, 58, 62
Athanasius, 26, 27
Augustine of Canterbury, 38, 44
Augustine of Hippo, 11, 12, 22, 23, 28, 29, 46, 48, 77, 82
Augustinians, 52
Austria, 81
Avignon, 55

Bacon, Roger, 53
Baius, 82
Balkans, 38, 39, 49, 62
Baptists, 72, 76, 88, 99, 100
Basil of Caesarea, 35
Becket, 55
Belgium, 82
Benedict, 43
Bernard of Clairvaux, 50, 52, 56
Bernard of Hildesheim, 54

Blandina, 16
Bonaventura, 65
Boniface of England, 45
Boniface VIII, Pope, 64
Borneo, 50
Bray, Thomas, 78
Britain, 11, 16, 18, 38, 81, 92, 97
Buddhists, 61, 94
Bulgaria, 59, 88

Calvin, 70f., 77
Campion, 80
Canada, 97
Cape Verde, 50
Capuchins, 80
Carey, 95
Carmelites, 52
Carthage, 12, 34
Carthusians, 52
Cathari, 53
Catherine of Siena, 66
Celsus, 20
Ceylon, 11
Chalcedon, 28, 39
Charlemagne, 38, 45, 46, 47
China, 38, 39, 42, 50, 61, 91, 93, 95, 97
Cistercians, 52
Claudius, 13
Clement, 22
Clovis, 35
Cluny, 39, 47, 51
Coke, 94
Colet, 67
Colman, 44
Columba, 44
Columban, 44, 45
Congo, 50
Congregationalists, 72, 97, 99, 100
Constantine, 18, 27, 31, 86
Constantinople, 27, 34, 37, 38, 39, 40, 41, 43, 46, 50, 58, 59, 62, 84f., 86, 89
Constantius, 18, 27

Cromwell, 73
Cuthbert, 44
Cyprian, 12, 29
Czecho-Slovakia, 49

Decius, 16
Denmark, 47, 49
Diocletian, 17
Dollinger, 83
Dominicans, 50, 52
Domitian, 13
Donatists, 12, 19, 29
Dunstan, 47, 54

East Indies, 91
Edinburgh, 98
Edward VI, 71
Egypt, 11, 21, 38, 42, 50, 59, 61
Elizabeth I, 71, 80
England, 39, 71, 72, 73, 74, 75, 78,
    81, 93
Erasmus, 67
Ethiopia, 11, 42, 59, 61
Europe, 93, 99
Eutyches, 27

Felicitas, 12
France, 11, 38, 45, 71, 75, 81, 82,
    90, 92
Francis, 44, 52-3
Franciscans, 50, 52, 79

Gaul, 16, 44
Germany, 38, 45, 75, 81
Goths, 11
Gottschalk, 46
Greece, 38, 39, 58, 88
Greenland, 49
Gregory I, Pope, 38, 44, 47, 90
Gregory VII, Pope, 54, 55, 57
Guinea, 50

Hadrian, 14
Hegesippus, 32
Henry II of England, 55
Henry IV of Germany, 55, 57
Henry VIII of England, 67, 71
Herbert, 72
Hildebrand, 54
Hinduism, 94
Holland, 45, 72, 81, 92
Humbert, 54

Hungary, 38, 49
Hus, 67, 92

Iceland, 49
Ignatius of Antioch, 15, 32
Ignatius of Constantinople, 41
India, 11, 39, 42, 50, 60, 91, 94, 97
Innocent III, Pope, 55
Inquisition, 53, 67, 79, 80
Iona, 44
Ireland, 11, 35, 38
Islam, 37, 42, 49, 50, 59, 60, 85, 90
Italy, 38, 39, 44, 58, 68, 79

Jansen, 82
Japan, 93, 97
Java, 50
Jerome, 31, 35
Jesuits, 80, 82, 85, 86, 87, 91
Joan of Arc, 66
John of Damascus, 40
Julian, 18, 19
Julian of Norwich, 66
Justin Martyr, 21, 22, 23
Justinian, 37, 39, 40, 41

Kiev, 49

Leo I, Pope, 34
Leo XIII, Pope, 83
Libya, 50
Liguori, 82
Lindisfarne, 44
Livingstone, 93
Lombard, 56
Loyola, 80
Lucar, 85
Lull, 50
Luther, 69f, 77, 79
Lutherans, 79, 97, 99, 100
Lyons, 16

Marcion, 23, 30
Marcus Aurelius, 15
Martin V, Pope, 63
Mau Mau, 95
Mary of England, 71, 81
Mesopotamia, 38, 49
Methodists, 76f., 92, 97, 99, 100
Mohammedanism, 61, 94
Monarchians, 25, 26
Monophysites, 39, 40, 42, 59, 61

Montanus, 24
Monte Cassino, 43
Moody, 77
Moravians, 75, 92
More, 67
Morocco, 50
Moscow, 62

Napoleon, 82
Nero, 13
Nestorians, 27, 42, 50, 60, 61, 96, 99
Newman, 78
Nicea, 26, 27
Nicholas I, Pope, 47
Nicholas II, Pope, 54
Nikon, 86, 87
Normandy, 38
North Africa, 11, 16, 34, 38
Norway, 45
Nubia, 42, 59, 61

Origen, 21, 22, 31

Palestine, 11, 38, 50
Pascal, 82
Patrick, 11
Paul, 13, 14, 20, 77
Paul of Samosata, 25
Pelagius, 16, 28
Perpetua, 12
Persia, 11, 38, 42, 50
Peter the Great, 86, 87
Photius, 41
Pietists, 75
Pilgrim Fathers, 73
Pliny, 14
Poland, 49, 81
Polycarp, 15
Portugal, 90
Presbyterians, 73, 97, 99, 100
Priscillian, 19

Quakers, 75, 99

Rahere, 58
Rasputin, 87
Robinson, 73
Rolle, 57
Rome, 11, 15, 16, 17, 33-4, 38, 46-7,
    56, 59, 62, 79, 83, 85, 87, 99
Rumania, 88

Russia, 38, 59, 62, 86, 87, 88, 95

Sabellius, 25
Salvation Army, 77, 99
Sankey, 77
Savonarola, 68
Scandinavia, 45, 47, 49, 81
Scotland, 11, 97
Septimius Severus, 16
Serbia, 59
Sicily, 38, 49
Spain, 11, 38, 44, 49, 67, 79, 81, 90, 92
Sudan, 38
Sumatra, 50
Switzerland, 70, 81
Syria, 11, 38, 42

Tertullian, 12, 20, 21, 22
Theatines, 80
Theodore, 44
Theodosius, 18
Thomas à Kempis, 66
Tibet, 50
Tolstoy, 88
Trajan, 14
Trent, 80
Tryggvason, 45
Tunis, 50

Ultramontanes, 82

Valerian, 16
Vandals, 12
Vienne, 16

Waldensians, 53
Watts, 77
Wesley, Charles, 77
Wesley, John, 76f., 92
Whitby, 45
Wilfrid, 44
William of Occam, 56
Williams, John, 95
Willibrord, 45
Wyclif, 67

Xavier, 91

Yugo-Slavia, 88

Zinzendorf, 92
Zwingli, 70